T. L. C.

Teach. Learn. Change.

B ARBARA D OUGLASS

Order this book online at www.trafford.com
or email orders@trafford.com

Most Trafford titles are also available at major online book retailers.

Printed in the United States of America.

isbn: 978-1-4907-3984-7 (sc)
isbn: 978-1-4907-3986-1 (hc)
isbn: 978-1-4907-3985-4 (e)

Library of Congress Control Number: 2014910735

Trafford rev. 06/12/2014

Trafford PUBLISHING® www.trafford.com

North America & international
toll-free: 1 888 232 4444 (USA & Canada)
fax: 812 355 4082

Acknowledgments

I wish to express my appreciation to my relatives and friends who thought I should write my teaching biography and ideas.
I especially was glad of the suggestions and technical help of Anna Brooks, Steven Douglass, Jan Santos, and Grace Zawitski

Introduction

When I was at university, there was no doubt in my mind about my future career. It would be in social work; I would work with children without parents; I would place them in good homes where they were wanted. My family—one grandmother, three aunts, one sister, one nephew, my father, my mother, and my goddaughter—are or were all teachers! Teaching was not to be my fate! It was just a routine, repetitive, almost useless, and frustrating job. There was a strong urge to be different, to really be able to contribute to the world! Considering the recent changes in society and all the single women who are raising their very much wanted children, there might not have been a social work future for me.

My mother argued with me, saying, "Since you will probably get married and never have to work, a teaching license could be useful. Your husband may die early. You can pick up the extra courses to get an education degree as you get your BA." I would retort, "But that will be so much extra work!" Finally, I was also encouraged by my father, who thought that I was so bossy that I would be a good teacher. I gave in. With protests, I did take the boring required courses and completed the BEd degree with the

BA. My parents were happy. As much as I now hate to admit it, they had been right! Do you not just hate it when that happens?

Not only that, but I did, as they predicted, get married and did, as I predicted, teach until I had a pension. When I took those education courses, I found they were easy to do and to work into my schedule. There had been one "good professor," Professor Love. He knew my parents, and he had even taught my mother. In his class we received the best pieces of advice. One idea of his was that since we might teach a long time, we would have happier, more successful careers if we were careful not to have the same year's experience thirty times. Talk about being naive! We laughed at his suggesting a long teaching career. Women at that time did not have careers. They had babies—many of them!

In this book, I tell how I actually did follow Dr. Love's excellent advice and did fulfill his prediction of having that long thirty-year teaching career. I was employed at many very different school locations. As you read about my good and the bad experiences, rest assured that all the names of pupils and fellow teachers have been changed. After that first awful and horribly stressful year, I had been married. I had even changed my own name. For this writing, I will be using my maiden name, Barbara Douglass. There are chapters about each of the many schools where I taught and about my necessary breaks I took. My best learning experiences involved both teaching situations and those breaks. It has been a fulfilling and wonderfully rewarding life. Undoubtedly teaching had been the best job for me and was where I probably did make my biggest contribution.

Before I begin the recounting of my teaching adventures, I am going to tell you a story of a person I met along the way. She was the inmate teacher, Alice. You will meet her at various times throughout the book. You will gradually realize why she is still, years later, an obsession in my thoughts and my prayers.

Alice's Story

The telephone rang. "May I please speak to Barb?"

"No. Sorry, she is still in jail."

The telephone rang again. "I would like to speak with Barbara Douglass, please."

"I am sorry. She is in jail. May I please take a message?"

"I am calling from her doctor's office. I didn't know the situation. When will she be out?"

"Probably by four o'clock this afternoon, I would guess."

"Would you please have her call us when she manages to get out of jail?"

These were not uncommon conversations for my husband to have while I was teaching at the Ontario Detention Center. The following conversation between the two of us was also not uncommon when I would return home for my lunch.

"I met the greatest person this morning. She has just joined our girls' class."

"Barb, she is a criminal!"

"But she is older, and she is going to help us teach in the room. She has been a professional teacher and can work with the girls who have reading problems."

"What is she in for?"

"Well, she has just done fifteen years in the special institution for women in Kingston [P4W]. She will stay at the West for months as she has a parole hearing and hopes to have her sentence reduced because of good behavior."

"OK . . . What was she convicted of?'

"Well . . . murder . . . but . . . well, just as an accomplice."

That was the first day I had met Alice, and I certainly did know her very well by the time she finally went to her patrol board hearing. She was like the many other women who came to the West while waiting in hope of a time reduction in the length of their sentences. She was as lucky as most of them. They were usually allowed to work because it was known that they would never cause trouble. Any incident would send them back to P4W immediately. They were usually the abused women whose husbands had been their victims. I heard their stories. Being a wife, I understood their emotional responses and the reasoning. I could not understand the horrible provocations that they had endured!

So began the developing relationship with Alice. Unlike those other women who had chosen work in the laundry, kitchen, or cleaning, Alice was one of the few to be allowed to use her professional training. I was especially glad as she was a big help in the summer when my classroom partner took his holidays. She could help with reading, crafts, and especially the computer. My skill there was almost nonexistent! She loved to talk. While we had very few things in common, we both had children. She had a foreign name and a foreign religion, and her children had been a long time with her parents in that foreign country.

It took many months, but I gradually learned her story as she gradually learned mine. How different those stories were! Her marriage had been arranged. I was married to the husband I chose. Her husband had been raised to believe his wife was his property. This attitude had led to the belief that he could treat her as he wished, using any form of abuse he wished. My husband never had the illusion that he owned me! She had been led to believe that her marriage was to be endured. I would not have endured. I had promised to obey my husband; that was part of the official service. Neither of us took that seriously! I did not need or want her details! She had been raised in a loving home. Her husband's treatment of her and of her two sons was psychologically too stressful for her to take. She called her parents; they came and took the boys to their home. That was, supposedly, to be for a short time so she could get some professional help.

From this point it developed into a situation that I had trouble even imagining. At that time she was still in Toronto and went to a well-known clinic. There was no emotional support from her husband, but other patients were helpful as were the therapists. I can vouch for this as I have had other friends who found this clinic to be a very real source of compassion and strength. She returned to her home with her unchanged husband. Now, she had her new friends for support. At this point, it all fell apart and the result was one dead husband and her murder charge.

The two accused perpetrators went to court. Her friend was found guilty of the murder. She was found guilty of being an accomplice murder. In her eyes she had been innocent. What would the parole board decide? Now fifteen years later, she was very hopeful of being reunited with her children and her aging parents.

Chapter 1

Seaview Regional High School (1959–1960)

Jan, a fellow graduate, and I had managed to get jobs in the same school, Symonds Regional High School. It was just outside Saint John, New Brunswick. We were feeling so excited, so scared, so "mature," and so lucky to have jobs. In reality, in those times and with those low salaries, they would have hired any willing person who had the qualifications who appeared to be breathing regularly. Teachers were not scarce! Our first trip to Saint John was to find a place to live. Dressed in our best tailored suits and wearing our girdles, we hoped we looked proper and responsible. We wanted to make a good impression on a lady lawyer who had advertised a flat to rent. She had planned to travel for the year; we needed it for a year. It was a pretty stiff interview. We got it!

Afterward, in celebration, we removed the girdles so we could be comfortable as we drove back to Fredericton in Jan's old blue Nash car. She had just purchased it for the grand sum of eight hundred dollars. That money had been her inheritance from her father, who had died many years ago. It was all that had been left when the lawyers were finished! That old Nash would be our regular means of transportation to and from school. We knew we were in for real adventures but never guessed that year would provide such great learning experiences. It was a very real contrast to the easy life of our four years in college! We learned, for example, that that the little car, while it ran on the cheap gas of the times, occasionally did not like to go. It was easy to push, fortunately, except up the steep hills in Saint John in a snowy, slushy storm. The owner was the driver. My mother had always said I was a big, strong girl!

That first day of school is just a blur in my memory, and Jan would say the same. The number of new faces was overwhelming. There were so many teachers and so many classes with so many students in each—names, names, and more names! Would we ever get them all straight? The important first job was to know each student's name so I could yell out to any miscreant. I had really done very little preparation for the actual courses, having not been given any outlines of what material to cover. I had just been handed the texts and been told I would be doing English, history, and health in grades 9 and 10. I bought a model of a human figure (not sexed). It came apart so we could all learn all the names of the bones and the organs. How hard could teaching health be? Of course, I was so confident that with my education and my good marks, I could do everything!

Was I in for a surprise? Fortunately, there were good and clear textbooks, but I was expected to teach *grammar*! That involved identifying parts of speech by putting various markings around each word. I had never done that in my life. I knew what a subject and predicate were, but how could one identify an adverb from an adjective? Preparations for classes really were going to take up a lot of the expected wonderful, anticipated spare time! Jan also found the preparation the same. I soon grew to be very envious of her. She taught math; it was easier and faster to correct. I learned that

that story would be the same for my whole teaching career. In the end, I was glad to be an English teacher as I loved the subject, and I liked being able to see when, though not often, a student's real appreciation was obvious.

By the end of my career, I was glad that I had been an English teacher. I had always loved reading stories but had not been too keen on the "good stuff" myself. The more I studied what I had to teach, the more I appreciated really good writing and most of the classics. I even learned to like poems without rhymes! In the upper grades especially, it was fun to watch as this same joy appeared for a few students. I was never naive enough to believe that I had inspired the whole class. There were, however, some very positive surprises usually revealed in private comments in my yearbook.

My real challenge was the history course. It was Canadian history, and we had never had that in the high school. There it had been boring British history, learning all those English kings and dates! Since then, I have learned a lot from fascinating historical novels. What a shame that it is verboten for students to get their history this way! History can come alive when one learns that these boring characters were very real people with faults and good traits. In my first teaching year, there was no time or enough understanding to be able to supplement appropriately the knowledge in that Canadian history textbook. My grade 10 history class was small and very quiet. At that time, their unquestioning listening was a real bonus. Later I realized that that was not good. Those who zone out are neither learning nor engaged.

One of those history students later became a well-known folk singer. Unfortunately, I had missed the valuable experience of getting to know an interesting, talented person. At this time I had no realization that students were immature but sometimes quite interesting people! I changed in that respect the longer I taught. This slowly acquired curiosity about other people's lives continues to be useful in retirement. I make an effort to remember it is not the person's words or even the body language but the eyes that convey the real message. That first year, one the boys in that grade 9 English class whom I did not read well was a real behavior problem.

This is a sad story. I had escorted the boy with the bad behavior to the principal's office. That man just looked at me and said, "I guess you'll have to strap him, won't you?" Since the boy was standing beside him, I had no choice. I had never been strapped and had never witnessed such an act, so I just did it as had seen it in movies. His hand got red, but he did not cry. I figured it was not hurting enough and kept on hitting. Finally, I just could no longer continue something that was so painful to me. The student left the room. That sadistic man said, "I thought you were going to kill the poor boy." Why did he not stop me? I gained from the experience; I learned never to expect the office do my discipline!

There were other trials as any new teacher will tell you. Meanness is not in my nature, but I had much to learn about self-control. I realized once that I was so upset that I was rapidly stamping my right foot as I yelled at the class. Fortunately, the humor of the situation became evident to me as I laughed. The class did too. The storm was over. It is so true that the mood and behavior of the teacher are instantly reflected in the students. Again, I was reminded that my main objective that year was class control.

I had one very real scare. The teachers had all been given a spiked stand on which to place the notes we received from the homes. It was on my desk at the front. I had encouraged the pupils to gather around there before class to tell me stories, having learned early how important oral expression was to writing skills. It was also a useful way to get to know them. To my horror, a boy put his hand on that spike, and it went through. He claimed it did not hurt and there was no blood. I choose to believe him. I hope I would never have done that today. It was wrong; that incident should have been reported!

Another big mistake was in my believing the IQ test scores, which were included in each student's school record. At college, it had been stressed that the teacher should study these records in order to know each student personally. We had been told that the IQ score of 100 was average. It had been stressed to us that we must know those records thoroughly, so I studied them. Many of my students had scored well below 100. In that case, I had been taught, I was not to expect much in the way of academic progress. How very wrong it was! Slowly, I have learned that my expectations usually set the achievement. Those old tests were based on culture as much as innate thinking ability. There were some pretty bright people in front of me. Some of them caught on more easily than I did to that stupid system of grammar markings! I will never know what might have been accomplished, in written work, for example, had my expectations been higher.

I had also wrongly based expectations of the comments written by elementary teachers. Obviously those ladies had experienced what is now common knowledge: Little girls usually behave better in the early grades and so are more "appreciated." Little boys suffer from what we now realize is the need for much more movement. One boy whom I know made very little academic progress until he was placed in a program that interspersed physical activity with sitting still. Frequent movement is a far superior "weapon" when compared with the use of drugs to keep active boys quiet. Either do that activity or let them start school a year later! Thus, for many of these boys, I did not have high-enough expectations. Later I learned never to look at records until I had formed my own opinions and had the students for quite a while. Each person deserves a clean new start.

Another trial occurred because I had understood it was important to take part in staff activities beyond the usual boring staff meetings. I had been asked if I wanted to take part in the weekly bowling team competitions. I agreed as I saw that as being friendly, and I hoped to make new friends. What a disaster! One poor group got stuck with me even though I had warned them that I had never bowled before. They valiantly soldiered on with me for the entire year. Did I learn anything? Well, I certainly neither learned to bowl nor liked the sport. Why? Well, I have since realized that I am not only dyslexic but also have dyspraxia.

In those days people had no idea of such a thing. I just figured that I was overly challenged in spelling and arithmetic and all sports. There I also learned that most teachers are wonderfully understanding and patient people. I would never join any team for any sport ever again!

And I loved to talk about clothes with the female students; it is still one of my passions. When I returned after Christmas with my engagement ring, the wedding became our favorite topic. Those were the days when that perfect dream was the gorgeous prince—and the "happily ever after" lie! The girls lived for that, though probably not as much as little girls do today since we now feed them a diet of the Walt Disney romance movies. Then, I did not discourage it as that was what I too believed. This would be my one and only year of teaching, and I too would be the happy housewife with a brood of children.

I realized what a good relationship I had established with the students when, later in June, the girls decided to have a wedding shower for me. They included my friend Jan, who was also soon to be married. The gathering was held after the exams at the home of one of my girls. It was fun and we teachers were very pleased. We received many individual gifts; I still believe that a lot of the mothers must each have sacrificed a china cup and saucer. This was not a wealthy area. We piled our precious gifts into Jan's old blue car and happily carried it all back to our flat.

That place still had to be cleaned and packed up as we were both moving. She was to be married in June, but I planned to travel to Europe and be married in September. My patient future husband had agreed to wait and had even loaned me his camera for the trip. I took many slides that are now fading away but have not been thrown out . . . yet.

Maybe I was not such a disaster as a teacher, after all. It was, I know, a year of mixed successes and failures. It was obvious that I had changed a lot and had learned a lot. I was so glad that I would never, ever have to teach again!

Chapter 2

West Island High School (1960–1961)

Wow! Here I was living the exciting life of a young person from Fredericton in the big city of Montreal! We went to nightclubs—a very big deal! I discovered I liked gin gimlets! Was I ever becoming sophisticated! I even saw a striptease show! *But . . .* where was that expected baby? I was stuck in a one-bedroom apartment with the only furniture in the living room being a trunk full of wedding gifts. I had to look for a job. My French was so limited that I could carry on only the politest of formal conversations. I read the job advertisements in the *Montreal Star.* I knew that I could not clerk in a store with such limited French! I had no office skills or skills with which to be impressive as an interviewee. I eventually did get one interview with the *Star.* Then I could not sell myself. That interviewer had been smart. Later, I found an advertisement for an English teacher at West Island High School. I was interviewed and was hired. I was to start right then, on the following Monday.

I began teaching at Lachine High School in November and taught there until June. It was so different from the dock area in Saint John. Lachine was a bedroom community for the English-speaking population who had very good jobs either in downtown Montreal or at the airport. The parent expectations were high, and the students were ambitious. There were almost no discipline problems. All pupils wore uniforms as they did in all government schools in Montreal. If the shoes or anything else was "wrong," that student was sent home to change. Are uniforms an aid to discipline?

There were definite course outlines for each class, and there were regular inspections of teachers. My classes were in grade 8 homeroom subjects and in grade 10 English. In Quebec at that time the high school started at grade 8 and finished with graduation at grade 12. That material required a lot of preparation, especially for the religion portion. Each year some Bible study was required, possibly to justify the parents' sending their child to a Protestant school. In the grade 10 classes, while working our way through the book of Proverbs, memory and discussion were required. That would be impossible now in the public schools. Have we become too sensitive about avoiding the potential for hurt feelings of people of other religions? I think it did not do those students one bit of damage. I was not casting my pearls before swine! The students were thinking. Bible studies also enrich the understanding of much of English literature.

Concerning personality difficulties with students, there is only one I can remember where I certainly learned, and I hope that the student did too. There was a super eager little girl who had been placed immediately in front of my desk and insisted on answering every question and obviously expected to be asked. By then, I knew enough to ration my attention and talk equally to all the pupils. She was not happy and asked to talk to me after school. I tried to help her understand that the desire to be always the center of attention and her acting so superior made her unpopular with the others. I told her I was really being kind in telling her what was happening. She carefully listened as I told her that from the front of the room I could see the negative effect of her behavior. I learned. Did she?

This was the first year that I can say that I enjoyed the companionship of the other teachers. Previously, I had been so scared to talk, so I listened and learned as those experts solved their discipline problems aloud! The art teacher, who was very beautiful, competent, and helpful to me, was so attractive that, if I had been her, I would have charged my superior with sexual harassment. Those were the days when females in any profession put up with oral references to their having sexually desirable features. At that time and at that age, I took those comments as insults. Now, at seventy-six, they would be gifts!

Probably the greatest test of my ingenuity that year was to meet the challenge of how to get from central Montreal to the suburb of Lachine. We could not afford a car, and even if we had had one, I am not sure we could have paid for the gas. There were buses and very long bus rides. While it did give me lesson preparation and marking time, it was a real pain as I get bus-sick! The principal eventually asked me how I got to the school. When I told him, he offered to give me a regular lift as he lived near to my apartment. I was very grateful, but he stayed at school later. How was to get home?

One day, while waiting at the bus stop, the guys who were delivering the *Montreal Star* to that paper box asked if I would like a ride into town. I said yes! And later I availed myself of their repeated offers to travel with them. I would find myself sitting in the back of the van on a pile of papers with my knees up to my chin. In those days, female teachers would never wear jeans, let alone slacks. Our skirts were very long and very decent! This newspaper truck was a rough ride but was okay as I was then starring at a couple of gorgeous, friendly hunks.

I was reminded of another piece of advice from Professor Love. He had asked us about who would be the most important people on the staff of any school we might be in. Most of us had assumed he meant the principal. He said, "No, it is the members of the janitorial staff and the office people whom you will depend on far more than on anyone else!" What words of wisdom again. Being friendly to everybody, especially to those delivery guys, had proved to be a godsend. This was another good lesson in humility and taught me that Integrity and kindness in any person were far more important in life than my having had the opportunity for a university education.

My husband was going to be transferred for his work to a plant in London, Ontario, where he would continue with the same company. After serious thought, he realized that he wanted to make a job change. He really preferred to go to Toronto as the prospects for future employment were more varied there. His application was completed for work as an engineer in a printing plant. The job was his and we moved to Toronto—still no baby! I was resigned to more teaching and now not quite scared and reluctant. What a surprise I was in for! Ontario actually had enough teachers! There was another problem to surface—I had not been educated in Ontario!

Chapter 3

Toronto No Job (Fall of 1961)

That's right—no job! I was not welcomed with open arms as I had been in both New Brunswick and Quebec. The Ontario Department of Education questioned both my qualifications and my health. They wanted Ontario teacher's certification and a certificate of good health.

I had realized the former might prove difficult but had assumed that my health was good. Surprise! The person I was sent to for a medical checkup decided that I had tuberculosis! A skin test said so. It took a long time to get that problem solved. There were special doctors to be seen to verify that the old needle skin test was a false positive. When finally I did get an x-ray, I was proven to negative for TB. Then on to solving the next problem— there was only one registrar, a lady named Jane, for all high school teacher certifications in Ontario. She was at the College of Education on Bloor Street. Finally, I was granted an interview, and she looked at my good college academic record and my precious two-degree certificates. Without even taking a deep breath, she just said no! Her problem with me was that I had taken too many courses in psychology and not enough in the so-called teachable subjects. I was told that, maybe, if I went to University of Toronto (U of T) and if I took and passed courses in each of English, history, and geography, then I might be reconsidered.

When I cooled down and started to talk with other people, I learned similar horror stories. My father, who had a BA degree and had later received his bachelor's in pedagogy from the University of Toronto, was similarly refused when he retired and had wanted a job here. The wife of a minister, who had a good postgraduate degree, had told us that she was able to work only in the elementary system. She suggested I try of go to someone she knew at the Provincial Education, Department of Education.

I must tell of one or two benefits of actually having this free time at a young age. My husband and I came to know Toronto and the subway system. We loved just going out to a parking lot near the old airport after supper just to watch the airplanes take off and land and to dream of such trips when we had more money.

That long-awaited appointment at the Department of Education for Ontario was finally granted. I joined the other out-of-province teachers who were waiting in the office. Holding all my certificates in my sweaty hands, I wondered what to do if I were refused. At last I heard my name. That director of education for Ontario looked at me, then looked at my papers, then looked at me again. I explained that I had changed my name when I was married. His smile grew broader as he said, "What did dear Jane do to you?" I explained the predicament. He wrote out a certificate so that I could teach in the elementary system. He told me that it applied up to and including grade 10. I was in business! My friend Alice had been luckier. She could just volunteer to teach in our classroom at jail. She had not even tried to get a teaching job after she was married and had moved to Toronto. With my new precious piece of paper in my hand, I signed up with the local boards of education. We had a car for my use to get to various schools to do supply work. Expecting only supply work, I began my long years of teaching.

Chapter 4

Supply Work in Toronto (1961–1962)

I was surprised by how many calls I received for supply teaching. I would accept a position from the first call I received each morning. What a variety there was! Most calls were for the younger grades. In truth, I had absolutely no idea of how to cope with the very youngest. It was the case of being the living, breathing, available body in the classroom. Usually, it did not take me too long to find the teacher's daybook, and if I was lucky, there was usually an outline of what *she* wanted me to do—almost no men teachers then! It was all fine as long as that lady had actually planned to be away on that specific day. A good teacher will leave her daybook with the following day's lesson plan in an obvious place.

One such job involved a grade 4 Class, and the teacher had written out the plan for the entire week; God bless her. Obviously it was for something that she had foreseen, like a health or family concern. It was also a class where there were absolutely no problems with discipline. The students were so well organized. We obviously had very different approaches to teaching. Even then, I believed that a little fun and spontaneity was needed. It was clear there must have been a lot of parental interest and involvement.

The greatest contrast to that "perfect" class was a kindergarten class in Weston. Thankfully, it was only for a couple of days. The modern early education classes are different. Pupils are sitting on a rug, or being at play stations, or playing a game for movement. Children at this early age do need movement, especially little boys. This teacher had left assignments and seemed to have encouraged the children to move just by coming to her after each little mark was put on the paper. I was walking around the class all the time. They needed not only a verbal confirmation but also a hug. With all the current concern about sexually harassment, this is forbidden. What a pity! How does any elementary teacher cope? The contrast between these two situations was the greatest. I was in many more classes with the common problem: the teacher did not have control or organization. No wonder she needed a day off!

North York Board of Education had the junior high school system (grades 7, 8, and 9). I went after Christmas to Beverly Heights Junior High. That time I had been working for a week in a portable with a grade 8 group. I was doing what was termed homeroom subjects, and the students were being good. I had been at it a few days and had been enjoying myself. In a portable, no one else hears what goes on!

That principal, an older gentleman, came in to watch the class and stayed for the next class also. In all my supply work, it was the first time anyone showed any interest in what I was doing. I had been out every day since acquiring that license! I honestly had wondered why nobody had bothered to visit. Did they just think that, if the room was reasonably quiet, I had survived? Did they decide to let sleeping dogs lie? Yet some of the classes were not as easy to control as dogs would have been! I hope today that it is different. Now, only the best new teachers even get the supply work. At the end of that class, the man asked me if I could sew. I looked at him and realized he was serious. I replied yes. He asked, "Would you like a full-time job here?" I hoped he heard in my voice the very real gratitude.

Chapter 5

Great Heights Junior High School (1961–1964)

That is right. I was employed at Great Heights Junior High. It was my very first real job in Ontario. Meanwhile, I continued working frantically to get the qualifications that were required for teaching high school. Gradually I took a course in English and one in history at University of Toronto in the summer school. The dreaded geography course was done at their night school. You will see that later this learning process was interrupted by the need to take other summer courses to qualify to teach family studies and to do guidance.

At Great Heights there were challenges. The area was what is now known infamously as the Jane-Finch Corridor. It was not as scary then but did, even then, have some serious social problems. We had a lot of subsidized housing and also some upper-middle-class homes. Only a few schools in those times had principals, such as this man. He thought the teacher was to enforce his/her own discipline. As a result, once I could establish the idea that I was the boss in the classroom, there was no questioning of my authority. For me this was a necessity, following my earlier resolve never again to send a student to the office for a strapping! I had learned.

At the outset, the most obvious difficulty concerned the head of the home economics department. She had been there forever and justly felt that she was the only living expert. Here she was stuck with me, a young inexperienced person who had absolutely no professional training in that field. In June at one of the infamous "promotion meetings," I began to realize why the principal had hired me. I witnessed their strong disagreement. He insisted that the student be passed on to the next grade. She refused as the pupil had failed cooking. It had been necessary in those days to pass all subjects to grade. He pulled rank and said, "She passes. It can't be that hard to make a lemon pie!" She was furious but patient with him.

I had been given couple of small home economics classes, and I had to be told everything that I was to do. Considering her situation, she was really extremely patient with me too. For each class, there was a lesson to be taught by the usual lecture method and a demonstration of how the product was to be made. In that semester, we were to do cooking—not my strength! So there I was, standing in front two classes, each with fifteen grade 9 girls. First, I had to act as the expert on how to make white sauce, having never done that in my life. My mother had never even made it. I would be asked, "Why are there lumps, miss?" The next day, they would be in small groups in their "own kitchens," making their own lumpy white sauce! By the end of my teaching career, I was so grateful to that boss. She had taught me so much, and we did eventually become friends; once I was no longer scared of her. I went on to take a series of summer courses to become sort of qualified as a person who could teach what was then called home economics.

I loved being with the students in a friendlier atmosphere, and the sewing section was what I really thrived on. Teaching home economics—and later, family living—made my whole working life a lot more palatable—figuratively and actually. Yes, I was learning, changing quickly, and surviving. Having taught the English before at the grade 9 level, it was much easier. I even had learned how to mark off various parts of speech! It was a pain and very difficult for some pupils. I was ready.

At first, it was all really a good learning exercise in my controlling me and hence gaining class control. I had learned by then the big clue was not to take anything personally, to be as fair as possible, and to use humor. Classes consisted of all boys or of mixed gender. The latter were easier. The outline for the grade 9 program said we were to study the play *Twelfth Night*. I would be merrily talking along and saying what I thought the words and scenes meant; the boys would all of a sudden break into loud masculine laughter. It was not a discipline problem; it was a problem of this teacher's being naive! I had had a Shakespeare course at university but never understood the amount of sexually explicit content he had used to keep his audience in the pit amused. The apprentices in the audiences of his time would have been standing there and drinking. They liked lots of sex and violence. Those boys taught me! When the gay man Malvolio is teased with the words said, "Board her, front her, assail her," it had nothing to do with ships! The laughter was a very bonding experience—meant figuratively!

The other classes were easier but again huge. School boards had to keep their numbers under forty. Those particular classes were usually at least over thirty-five. Our salaries were still not good. The Teachers Federation gathered strength as I continued working, and pay scales improved. Even with these large student groups, we were able to have good class discussions about the topics in the stories. At the end of the first June, a group of girls wrote me a lovely letter of appreciation, saying it mattered so much to have a person with whom to talk about things of concern in their lives. I still have the letter!

There was something I could not say to them that was a concern of mine. One bright beautiful girl was not planning to return to school for grade 10. She was to be married in the summer to an older man who was building her a lovely new house. She was just almost fifteen! The other girls thought that she was the luckiest person. She could have her own house and have babies! Was that not their purpose in life? I had been as trapped as they then were in that myth. I could only say what my situation was I was married, I had no baby, but I had a job I liked.

Staff room gossip usually was the source of formation about other social problems. There was one tale of a boy whom we had all found difficult. His father, in a drunken rage and fit of religious fervor, had attempted to nail him to a wooden cross—*and* he was expected to behave normally in school! One horror story concerned a girl in one of my English classes who had not attended regularly. I found out why when I had coffee with my cousin who was her social worker. Her economic situation was so desperate that they had found her a factory job, and she was granted special dispensation to work at an early age. That was not the whole story. She had been working as a prostitute. The factory job was sorting screws—funny, if it had not been so tragic.

It was here also that I stayed long enough to really get to know my fellow teachers and to feel comfortable about asking for advice with classroom problems. I then felt that I was not working alone. The principal was also approachable. The head of the English department was a great help. She taught me how to set up and value exam questions; I had never done it before. I had great respect for her. It was not too long before we were friends, a friendship that continued after she retired. We visited back and forth, and she and her partner had visited our home more than once.

There were also staff parties while I was that school— segregated by sex, of course! At these ladies' parties I enjoyed myself, and I got to know some ladies well. I was one of the few working wives—again it was symbolic of the times. I mention all this because it gave rise to a mystery. One lady had had a lot of incidents where she had had things stolen from her apartment and from her car. Once, that happened when we were all gathered at her place. She gave a good party, and we all had enjoyed ourselves until, upon leaving, a couple of women found that their purses had been rifled. Their wallets had been taken. What a shock! Of course, we were all suspicious of each other. She reported it to the police. It turned out that they had been watching her. She was arrested. Did she ever go to jail? Would she have ever volunteered to teach with us as Alice did? Not likely. There had been other teacher inmates who had no interest in helping our girls.

To my delight and surprise, I was then asked to be the head of English at a brand-new school, Emery Junior High School. Those two and a half years at Beverly Heights were serious learning and changing experiences. I was happy, awed, and enthusiastic about my new challenge.

Chapter 6

Morris Junior High School (1964–1966)

I was still in the junior high school system. I had just passed one required home economics course and had the low C in the dreaded geography. However, I did not have that needed certificate required to take the special course to be able to teach high school the Ontario way. That would happen in the next summer. I was glad to work the summer of 1964 to prepare the course outlines and the English texts for the new school.

That first summer at the new Morris Junior High School, I spent acting like a boss. I was very impressed by *myself!* Here I was, a relatively new, young teacher, and had been given the responsibility of being an *English head*. It did not take too long to realize that there was really a lot to do for an extra thousand dollars a year! I did, however, like the responsibility of making my own adjustments to the official courses and of deciding exactly what the official statement of "my" department policy would be. I was in this new school a lot and had limited holidays. It taught me the necessity of work-life balance if one is an administrator.

T. L. C.

Though I was later asked to consider administration, I chose to remain a plain, ordinary teacher. Being a boss involved grunt work, as well as teaching and administration. Those English texts all had to be ordered, stamped, and put on the shelves in our storeroom. I believed I was totally ready for the first day and for the first staff meeting. I was nervous! I was important! Remember, though, this was in the sixties when almost anyone with a good education could realistically have any teaching job!

The Morris student population was quite similar to that of school I had just left but not as balanced socially. Most of these pupils lived in subsidized housing. Their backgrounds in English were varied as well. Obviously, in most homes, there had been no extra money for newspapers or books. The children were eager to learn, and the parents were relatively supportive. I still had not really learned the value of home contact. I wish now that someone in teacher education had stressed the importance of parental involvement. That is something that most teachers still do not understand. Later in my career, I did it a lot of the phoning and even visiting. I was frequently told, "We have never heard from a teacher in years. We had no idea he/she should do homework."

Pupils from the Morris area rarely, if ever, left to explore other parts of Toronto. I know this because the North York Board of Education once a year would take our students by bus to the Old Massey Hall. It was for a concert put on by the Toronto Symphony Orchestra. They learned a lot more than music appreciation! As the bus went through the downtown area, there were loud exclamations. "Did you see that really high building?" "Hey! Look at that girl!" "Oh, that is where Sam the Record Man is!" Once they left the bus, the heads were tilted back to look up at the skyscrapers. It is the way I feel now when downtown.

At Morris, I was given some time for student counseling. I did not have any official documentation to prove I was a counselor. I appreciated the chance, and it did not take long before I was busy. The guidance head there was a man of whom I grew very fond. He had served in the war. He insisted my husband and I visit his home for a meal and to meet his wife.

It was also in that situation that I came really to understand the need of teens to be able to talk to someone older, someone who was not their parent, someone who had not been yelling at them all their lives. Their questions were easy, and I could only hope not to contradict what the parent might have said. I particularly remember one girl in grade 9 who wanted to know how a baby was able to get out of the mother's tummy when the time came for him to be born. I had to say that I honestly did not know. That was no help! It would have been better to have asked her why it was that she needed to know about babies. Did she need help? A lot of the facts learned about the pupils were revealed after school. There were no school buses. They walked. We could keep them after class to discuss problem behaviors. I had the confidence to talk with the students as most of my undergraduate classes had been in psychology. I was an expert! Yes, right! What nerve one has when one is young!

The students did seem comfortable with me, and that really saved me more than once. I had one group of grade 9 girls who were at the general level. We were to study a scene from *Julius Caesar*, and I planned to play a recording for them. It was the takeoff by Wayne and Schuster of Calpurnia beseeching Caesar to stay home. She had the premonition of his death. I had been late coming to class. When I finally appeared, having found the record player, they were all gathered around the desk. We all were excited and we listened there at the desk as a group. After a while of listening and laughing, one of the girls asked me why there was a man sitting at the back of the room. I panicked! I had forgotten that the official inspector was to be in the school some time soon. There he was! I was smart enough not to be too obvious. We continued for a few more minutes until the scene was finished. Then, I told them what the writing assignment was. They took their seats, and I introduced the man.

I did not, but I could have, hugged him when he told me he was pleased with the teaching and with the warm and friendly atmosphere in the room. Some of the old fogies I had had as inspectors would have given me a very poor rating for being late and for not having the pupils all sitting properly in the neat rows of seats. Such a poor rating would have been with me forever, and I might have had to change careers. We used to joke in the staff room about how the promotion system for all administrators was for those who could not teach. I honestly had one man later who wrote in his report that I had made a grammar error on the blackboard. I know I did not because I rarely used the board because my spelling was so poor!

It was at that school at lunchtime that I learned to enjoy playing various card games and to perfect my bridge skills. Thus I became friends with more people. It was also the school where, as I mentioned before, it was acceptable to have mixed staff parties; we had some really great times. There were the golf tournaments (when very few of us really knew how to golf) and house parties.

Our principal there was very approachable. He remained a friend, especially after he retired and he and his wife joined our church. There were several of the members of that staff with whom we kept in touch. One lady and I are best friends and have been there for each other all these years. The same applies to one of the wives whose husband has since died. She and I went through the experience of new knees together recently. The vice principal was of the old school and scolded me severely for suggesting to him that a student I knew about might benefit from his counsel. Change can be slow!

I had finally learned that my parents were correct: teaching was probably the right job for me, and I was happy. Here, I really liked my fellow teachers. I believe it was because we were all young in relation to those I had met in the other schools. None of us were set in our ways, and we were open to enjoying life. I expect that the inspector who liked me had found the same joy and good feeling in the other classes also. I am so upset now when I hear about all the eager new graduates who have their hearts set on this career and have trouble finding even the most difficult classes for supply work. My one recurrent nightmare is one in which I have been called upon to do supply work, and I am not able to find the rooms. The building is huge, and as the time bells go, I am running all over in a panic. Is this the scene for some of our new potentially good teachers?

Just as I was looking forward to another year at this comfortable place, my husband decided to change positions. He had been working as a plant engineer but realized that he did not want to spend the rest of his life there. His application to study for his masters in business at the University of Western Ontario had been accepted.

We were off to London for September. It was exciting, especially since it proved easy for me to get a teaching job at the grade 9 level in English. Again inadvertently, I was doing as Professor Love had advised—not working in a comfortable rut! I would face a whole new set of challenges. I would, however, be working in a real high school environment.

Chapter 7

Montgomery High School (1966–1967)

This date would imply there was only there for one school year—not true. Actually it was for the fall of 1966 and spring and fall of 1967 as well. Thus, it was a year and a half. Grade 9 English classes were the courses I was teaching. I was forced to stop at Christmas of 1967. Why? Was I really a failure in a high school setting? No—I was pregnant! That much wished for baby was on the way! What a surprise! We were very happy and excited. In those days one did not discover the sex of the child until birth. Who would it be? I enjoyed the mystery. I had been supposed to teach for those two years while my husband studied for his MBA. In that fall, the principal wondered if maybe I could continue with our infant in a basket on the desk. It was a nice compliment, but I knew he was not serious. We had a little in savings, thank goodness. We also had faith that there would probably be a good job for my husband when he graduated in the spring. That meant a lot of pressure on him because we were of that common sixties belief: a mother never works, especially when her child is not of school age.

With trepidation, I went into my first experience as a real high school English teacher. The College of Education registrar had told me I did not have enough English literature courses in my background. Knowing I had to keep busy and that my husband would have a heavy study load, I took an English course for a credit. We had then decided that we would check into the possibility of an adoption at the end of the second year. We did indeed want children but had by then given up hope of our own.

I was soon well established at Montgomery Side Road. I had discovered that I really loved being a teacher. Having been given only grade 9 was fine with me. The older students looked pretty big, and my grade 9 pupils were new to the high school and probably more scared than I was. There were no discipline problems that I recall, and the level of reading varied as to whether or not they were in advanced level or general level. There were not many parents at parents' nights. I still no reason to phone parents—bad mistake!

At Montgomery Side Road, I do remember pupils being kind to me, particularly when I had such a time learning to pronounce their foreign names. It was a time when a lot of people were coming from Italy. There was one small boy with the name Pasquale, and he had to help me repeatedly. I felt so incompetent and so sorry for him. Their kindness became yet more evident later. That first year there passed smoothly and I enjoyed my time in the school. Late in the spring there was, however, the pregnancy. In summer, I made huge tent dresses for myself and had started to wear them early in September to fool the students. For a while I thought I that I had such a good job of it. By November, I figured it was time to say something. I know how upsetting it is to find that the teacher is leaving halfway through the year. There were the usual expressions of surprise, but one grade 9 boy turned triumphantly said, "See, I told you so!"

I taught until school closed at Christmas. I had to sit down a lot more to check progress. I usually walked around the room and marked their work at their desks. I can only remember their never taking advantage of the situation—or did they?

There is one relevant student story. In the fall, a boy who had left London and gone to live in Detroit came back to see me and to tell what his new school was like. First though, I asked him how he had made out because that had been a summer of the terrible riots in Detroit. He said that he had lived right downtown and had had the job of sitting on the front doorstep with a loaded rifle across his knee. He had been the protector of his family. Great kid! He also told me that, since I had suggested he repeat grade 9, their school had tested him. They had placed him ahead by two grades! I really did not question my own assessment but chocked it up to different educational standards.

If I remember correctly, there were a couple of baby showers given by the ladies—no mixed parties here! These were much appreciated but a little tame! The staff relationships had been well established when I arrived, and so there was never one member with whom I became a particularly close friend. Again, I would like to suggest that this could be the situation now in many schools. New teachers are rare. There is no place like a staff room for cliques.

Although expected by everyone to be early, our daughter did not arrive until February. I had lots of very necessary help when she finally put in her noisy appearance. Was I content? Yes, because we had our long-awaited baby. No, because I had learned to appreciate, and did miss, the joys of teaching.

In spring there was the expected job and a move to Toronto for life in another rented townhouse. Fortunately, other couples from the MBA course with whom we were friends rented homes near us. The boys were so busy getting established in their wonderful new and challenging jobs that we rarely saw them. We women still met for coffee and baby talk. A new lifestyle! A year later, we moved into our own bungalow, with its 9 percent mortgage. I missed teaching and the contact with the pupils. What I really had difficulty with was the need to develop patience. I knew that I could control and manage a class of rambunctious teenage boys. This little girl, who weighed less than twenty pounds, had me bamboozled! Change was needed indeed!

Chapter 8

Homeschooling? (1968–1975)

H ere, I am not using this term as most people nowadays understand it. I did not use any material that was on the elementary school curriculum for Ontario. I was aware that what I was really teaching this time was readiness for school. My friends who had taught in elementary grades assured me that if a child arrived at school knowing how to read or to do simple arithmetic, he/she would be the bane of his/her teacher's existence. Not only that, the child would be bored, would cause problems, and would learn to hate school. One boy whom I know well had actually taught himself to read before kindergarten. He had to be placed with in all-girl class to keep him even a bit interested and quiet.

My aim, therefore, was to keep my own sanity and hopefully to help develop the bright mind, which I, like all mothers, imagined my child had. I was fortified by the thought that brains of any ilk could be improved with stimulation; so I proceeded to overstimulate! Long before she could possibly understand, I talked incessantly. I tried not to use a threatening voice, but not everything I said was very loving, especially when she cried in the middle of the night!

When the talking started, I heard repeated many of the things that I had said. There were some surprises too! I had been reading books of poetry to her, and she seemed to appreciate the rhythms. That, as an English teacher, pleased me. My favorites were poems from my childhood book by Robert Louis Stevenson. The biggest surprise came when my husband and I had gone to view a river that was in flood. From the little person in the car seat came the words "Dark brown is the river, golden is the sand . . ." etcetera. One never knows how much is being absorbed.

In those early years, children have very little in their heads. If the hearing is good and if they are the least bit observant, it all registers. Maybe reading and language are not your things. This is also the stage to encourage all activities. If you are a singer, an artist, or an athlete, teach your thing. I could not believe how early my sister had her girls on skis. My daughter and I had a lot of fun just on our walks to the plaza. It could take a long time. If I were buying groceries, then the store would deliver, so there was no rush. We might sit on a lawn or on the curb and discuss and examine bugs and rocks. There were a lot of questions, and if I did not know the answer, it was a chance to engage imagination! "Mummy doesn't know the reason. What do you think?"

One of the best things about the plaza was that there were a lot of other shops besides the grocery store. We usually had to visit the jewelry store, which was also the post office. That meant that she was allowed to lick the stamps for each letter! She learned to speak with adults. The jeweler, the druggist, and especially the ladies in the bakery all became friends. It was also great for me to be able to talk with adults. I had a couple of ladies on the street with whom coffee was a regular necessity; they too had children the age of mine. One on them is still a very important to me; the other was a smoker and had died.

Now, it seems it is even necessary to prearrange playdates. For us, they were just automatic as there were so many other children on the street. They did the organizing. Some of the older ones even put on plays for the little ones. I remember one girl who could barely walk attending the performance in the nude as she did not like her wet diaper. It was a hot day! One childless man and his wife gave the children treats and loved having them visit. I guess it is now obvious that the street looked after the socializing of my daughter. We only enrolled her in a formal nursery school for a couple of months before she began kindergarten. I wanted to see if she could cope socially. She could.

Take the ideas suggested in this entire chapter with the knowledge that it was the sixties, and I had only one child and the help of many neighbors. I was in a most fortunate time and place. It must be impossible nowadays to do too much of your own school readiness preparation.

Chapter 9

Haifa High School (1975)

In December 1974, with my child in the public school system, I answered an advertisement in the *Globe and Mail*; I got the job. I was not prepared to work full-time, but this position would be in the afternoons, and I would be doing the familiar grade 9 English. In the summers, I had finally taken the course to be qualified to be an Ontario high school teacher. Now I knew how to teach the Ontario way! Next, I decided to take more English courses to become eligible for the English specialist certification.

It may seem a puzzle to hear that I worked just one year at this school. I did one spring and one fall. Then I was offered a permanent job with the Etobicoke Board of Education. The Haifa High School had been kind enough in the fall to increase my job time and pay, but the temptation to have a full salary was too much. Our mortgage was by then 13 percent! I was sorry to leave the Jewish school as I had had a lot of fun there, and it was so different from anything I had experienced. I hope that I can do it justice here and tell of all the interesting things that I learned. For the parents, there was a lot of tuition to pay, and I know of some parents did not have a lot. They had decided that a cultural and religious education would benefit their children. If I had been Jewish, I would have sent my child to Haifa High School, no matter how hard I had to work to do it. The school hours were long, except for the early Friday closings in the winter. There were many classes in Hebrew and Old Testament. There were more academic subjects than were studied in public schools.

This variety of courses meant there were many different teachers with many different backgrounds. The male teachers of the Hebrew subjects were obviously very conservative. Some always wore hats, but there were none of the very unusual costumes I had seen in Israel. That trip to the Holy Land and my reading of the works of writers such as Eli Wiesel were real eye-openers. I fully realize it is important for all children to know their cultural backgrounds. Our daughter got an overdose of bagpipes! Here, there were obviously different teaching styles. The first time I was in one of the classrooms used by a rabbi, I was shocked; he had been smoking as he taught. His ashtray had been the main drawer of the teacher's desk. I just asked the students if this was normal. It was! We opened the windows for a while and straightened up the higgledy-piggledy desks. Then, when we all could breath, we started!

Later, they told me what they had done to one poor English teacher who had not quickly gained control. He had found himself hanging outside from the second-story ledge. They had all departed for their own self-made recess by exiting the same way. He had attempted to follow! I thus was warned; it would be necessary to gain instant respect. That was soon accomplished for both classes.

I quickly realized that if the parents were paying, they would want to know how the English was progressing. The students honestly were the best I had ever taught. There was such pressure on them. It was most gratifying to have parents' nights there. The parents knew what they wanted and were appreciative that

I delivered. Yes, I met fathers and mothers with their tattooed numbers, some very large and some smaller. I was most humbled. In saying that those students were the best, I am referring to both behavior and study habits. The homework was always done; one boy even had Daddy's secretary type up the essay! Did she correct the spelling? I will never know. Even the class that had all boys was easy. There were a couple of students at the back who were larger and obviously planned to attend university. They wanted no nonsense. I had always had the system that, if I was passing back the marked work, I would explain how I had allotted points. Any personal questions would be taken up individually after class. When one of the smaller boys with a snoopy of his kippa decided to argue, I just kept repeating that mantra. Finally, one of those big boys said, "Oh, for goodness sake, shut up. If you don't, she'll think we are all as bad as you!"

It did not take too long to realize that these pupils had all been together since their first days at kindergarten, maybe even in nursery school! They had spent their summers at the same residential summer camps. Talk about knowing each other's personalities and quirks! All classes used to be in that same old building on Bathurst Street. It was the same familiarity for the staff. Most of them had only taught at that school. They were friendly to me and I was invited to the ladies' gatherings. There I heard a mixture of Yiddish and English, and they were quick to change if it might seem that I was being left out. They were very kind to me. Again, I was humbled as I cannot even carry of a conversation in French, which I have supposedly studied.

The most humbling experience of all was the day I came to school and discovered it was the celebration of the festival of Esther. There was food and drink. There were no classes; the students were there to party with the teachers! It was a giant celebration and some of the teachers were really having fun. No problem, I love a party! There was dancing in the gym; I heartily entered the spirit of the day. I joined a big circle of my boys and had danced until I was tapped on the shoulder. "Barb, girls can't dance with the boys. You go over there!" I laughed. Then realized the person was serious! Red face—you bet!

Another real learning experience happened when one of the men on staff was getting married. His special friends were all invited to the actual ceremony, and the rest of us who had collected for a common wedding gift went to the celebration known as the sweets table. I love sweets; it could not have been more impressive to me. Never in my life had this poor goy seen anything like it. The bride's father owned a bakery. That display may have even impressed some of the other teachers. I had been invited to bring my husband, and it was the type of thing we still talk about. The two sweets-laden tables were arranged in arcs, facing each other. The bride and groom had pictures taken standing between them. Each table contained identical desserts at exactly the same location on each. It was a riot of color, of shape, and when we tasted, of flavor as well.

When I started there again in the fall, I had the longer hours. The school situation felt very much like home and I was really enjoying myself. It was just a given that the first few minutes of class would be spent tidying the room and that they would help and then get to work. When I had to tell them before Christmas break that I would be leaving, they seemed genuinely chagrined. I was taken aback as I thought I had been seen as a bit of an ogre. For the last time of each class, students had organized a surprise party. It was much more than I expected or deserved, and there was one big gift from each of the classes. There was a gift from the staff fund as well. That one was for a smoker; it was an ashtray with "product of Israel" stamped on the bottom. It continued to be my favorite until I stopped smoking.

Did I change as well as learn? I do not like clichés, but this one was true: it is so obvious to me how wrong, how very wrong, it is to continue to judge a person by the group with whom he/she is identified. I met many wonderful people at Haifa High School. Although I was the person who was not of their group, I also was judged as normal—even with all the faux pas I had committed!

Chapter 10

Tolton Collegiate Institute (1976–1978)

Finally, I was officially licensed and employed as a high school teacher. Tolton was a good school with a reputation for high academic standards. It was supposed to be the best place to teach in Etobicoke. More importantly, I could walk to work. That meant that we could survive a little longer with one car in order to get that mortgage paid off.

The two and a half years here passed quickly and pleasantly on the whole. The classes were easy. In one, I was greeted the first day by a sign on the blackboard. It said, "No more Mr. Smith!" Pretending not to understand, I quickly erased it. That group certainly did not give me any trouble. Another class was so quiet even I could not stir up any fun! It was all work, work, work, and more work. One of those girls I now see frequently because she is my dentist. I also consider myself a friend, so I asked her if she had been as bored as I had. She told me no. How good is her memory?

Life became more interesting and challenging when I was asked to be in the guidance department. The department head was very well organized, which meant I was told exactly what to do. It was basically academic guidance. We saw each student in each class each year. For the grade 9 pupils, we saw them also in September to ask how they liked being in high school and if there were any difficulties. The feeder schools helped us, and we often had special pupils flagged to see first. I was called to the principal's office for one such case. We had been told to watch for the girl's trouble with French. I had offered her a list of French tutors. Her mother had panicked. She came into school, and I had to apologize to her and to the child for even suggesting such a problem. Was I caught? Yes! The parents were not supposed to know about the other school's reference.

I found formal guidance challenging because I had done so much informal talking with students. I hoped I might finally make use of my university background. I enjoyed it and started taking enough summer courses to meet the requirements for my guidance certification. I did not, however, use it again until I was teaching in the jail system with my friend Alice! At this school, when talking to each student, it was mainly about his/her choices of subjects for the coming year. I was to ask for any problems and about career plans. The grade 9 girls were often planning to be veterinarians; they loved their pets. The boys just said "I don't know" and sat wriggling and looking awkward.

There was one surprisingly confident grade 9 boy with perfectly combed hair. He had his academic life totally planned. His father and he even knew what he would be studying in each of the next several years. After talking with him, I came home and told my husband that I had just interviewed Canada's future prime minister. We laughed and wondered again about the ambitions of young people. We laughed again and marveled when he was elected to that post! At this writing, he is still our prime minister! Basically, we think he and his finance minister have guided our country through some pretty rough seas. I have now come to understand the power of determination and the value of loving, supportive parents. For some people, it just takes time to reach goals. I have seen it with people who are very determined to be medical doctors. There are so many routes, if one has determination.

Occasionally, a student I had been teaching would ask to see me just to talk. One case, about which I still occasionally worry, involved a conference not only with the student but also the parents. He had not been doing well academically. He had been adopted and they did not have much background information. Proudly, the father bragged about how skillfully the boy could take the large family cruiser into the dock. The mother was most proud of the way he had played tennis and could defeat everyone his age and older at their club. It was just the marks they were worried about. I asked gently if they could afford a private school. Indignantly, they both said, "Of course." I followed that interview with research about private schools in the area, and I found one to recommend. There the discipline would be strict. Going home for visits was a reward for academic success. The parents sent him there for the next year. I never heard how he made out.

While most of this area was upper middle class economically, a few were not. One boy had serious difficulties. He had run away from home more than once, and the courts had placed him in a residence for difficult-to-manage teens. I visited him there, and he really was happier. The rules were strict. I was able to bring him some of his course material. How did he eventually make out? Another English student from grade 11 had come after school to talk to me about the problem of his mother's alcoholism. All I could really do for him was to listen and try to help him to understand where his mother was coming from. I asked about her community volunteer work; I stressed its importance. He had told me of the pain she lived with. Did he feel better? I hope so. Then, he gained a friendly girlfriend, and he and she had great fun on his motorcycle.

I had one genuine classroom scare in this school. When I had entered a grade 9 classroom after lunch, there was a fight in progress. I was strong, and my teacher voice was stronger! I broke it up. I was able to send one participant to his seat. The one who wanted to prolong the fight, I pinned against the blackboard. He was a fairly well-known tough little hockey player and stronger than I. It was a great relief to see a colleague who came running to my door. He escorted the child to the office. Later, he told me he was surprised at what I had done; so was I!

One of my best classroom experiences here was the time I was given a grade 10 history class to teach. I had believed there was a fair bit of freedom for the teacher. Given the topics to be covered, I took it as my chance to decide just how to approach each area of study. Reading about the past was interesting to me. I had ideas that I hoped would make the class better than by just using the usual lecture method. The class was supposed to study of Canada from Confederation to present. Topics included immigration, the two wars, and understanding the parliamentary system.

First, I asked the students to research how and when their own ancestors had come to Canada. I am not sure just how their families reacted, but the pupils had fun. It forced them to talk to their living grandparents and/or even some great-grandparents who were alive. One boy found that there was an old trunk in the attic that the family had never really looked at. In it was a journal telling of the ancestors' trip to Kitchener from Pennsylvania in a Conestoga wagon! Quite a few of the students discovered that they had Ukrainian ancestors. Since we had been supposed to look at the settling of the western provinces of Canada, those reports were a godsend. One girl had even been back to the Ukraine with her family to see and understand why they had come here. I told them of my family's settling and of clearing land in New Brunswick in the 1800s. There were others of similar backgrounds.

We had mock sessions and debates like those in government. We set up the room with rows of seats facing each other on the two sides of the room. We debated such topics as whether or not Quebec should be allowed to leave Canada. I introduced news stories, such as René Lévesque's health since he was a serious smoker! It was fun, but it did get rowdy. Does that not sound like the House of Commons?

When it came to the topic of the Second World War, we had parents who had actually been in that war visit the class as speakers. The father of one boy in the class had even been a paratrooper who had been dropped behind the lines into France. He had kept the supplies he had been given and showed them to us. He even had the suicide pill that he had he had been given to swallow if needed! One girl had a stepfather who had fought on the German side. He was aware of the possible prejudice he might face, so he just sent in a tape on which he talked about what he had gone through. It really gave a good view of the suffering that there was on both sides! I told them of the air raids that I had lived through as we had been living on the east coast of Canada. I could add human interest. I was a child, so I suffered from lack of candy! There was no rubber for elastic in underwear! I had had a life without my father for five years when I was young. Did they enjoy that class as much as I did? Needless to say, I was not to teach that course ever again!

Because I am a good listener, and the students came to talk after class. I heard about some of the spectacular house parties that were held when the parents were away. That was a signal for all friends to gather, with their stimulants at that home. Afterward, they would tell me about the many dollars of damage, the arrests, and the alcohol-poisoning escapes.

Believe me, the staff parties were tamer than the students' gatherings. I remember ladies' get-togethers but none of note that included men. I remember the men did have times when they went curling or did some sport together. There was one outstanding staff incident when a male teacher was arrested. He was then made to spend his time at the board office until he could go to court. Unlike the case of Alice, if people have the money, they do not have to wait for their court appearance in a detention center. They merely wait at home, or as in this man's case, even continue to collect their pay! He had been accused of being the truck driver in a gang. They had been stealing goods from warehouses by hitching that cab to a parked loaded trailer. Later, I heard a person in the staff room say he had wondered how the man was able to sell calculators so cheaply! He did not suffer as did Alice.

Many staff members had been in that school for years and years, and some had even taken their own high school education there and returned to teach after university. They were friendly and not in cliques. There were interesting discussions. One expert in ancient history allowed me to sit in on his lectures as I had never known much on that topic. That was much appreciated and most generous.

My life here was going smoothly until the great teachers' strike of 1977–78. Most of these teachers walked out and stayed out all of December and most of January. I did not join them. I will explain first what the rationale was for the walkout. My father had taught and had been a principal all his life. He had had the prestige. We lived on his meager salary or what he could earn on odd jobs in the summer. At retirement, his pension was five thousand dollar a year. He had to go to work for another ten years so he and my mother could live and could educate his last two children. Yes, I was glad that there were unions in Ontario. Even more money sounded good to me as it did to the others. There were always class size issues and other work problems as well to be negotiated.

To fully appreciate the union's position, we were all invited to a huge city-wide meeting at the old Maple Leaf Gardens. It was packed. The leaders were on stage and the band was playing. I had decided to sit in the bleachers as my mind had not been entirely made up. Because of my background, I was aware of the power of mob psychology. I sat with another staff member who also had not yet decided to join the strike. We watched and learned; wow, did we learn! It was calm at first as we heard the anticipated explanations. Then the chairperson spoke. She was an English teacher, and it soon became obvious to me that she had modeled her oratory on the speech Mark Antony had used to turn the people against Brutus. She used those clever devices to turn her audience against the board's offer. Apparently, this was not as obvious to teachers sitting in front of her. Soon they were all singing "We shall overcome!" We were shocked. Could I have been singing along had I been sitting among the others? Who knows? As I said, I was fully conscious that teachers should be adequately paid. The rumor, however, seemed to be that there was an adequate offer in the works. The friend with whom I had sat had had severe reservation about the idea of being involved in civil disobedience. I believed I had the right to make my own decision.

Knowing that I would not sit at home, I had to make my position clear. It would involve crossing the picket line, which was actually done the first day but not thereafter. I really respected the right of the others to picket, and I wanted them to know that I was not critical of their actions. Just before they walked out, I decided upon a solution. Each of the seventy-seven teachers would get his/ her own handwritten letter from me explaining my stand and why I was in the school. I did not want anyone to think the board was sponsoring me. I assured them that my money, after taxes, would go to charity. The money from my December paycheck went to the Salvation Army. The January check put a new pew into the little Anglican church in Cow Head in Newfoundland. My brother-in-law was the minister there. Honestly, the only reward I received was the knowledge that I was following my conscience.

The teachers ended their strike near the end of January. As they returned, their responses to me were mixed. I fully understood those who chose not to speak and those who only wanted the whole mess behind them. One lady even suggested that I should have regularly brought coffee out to them. If I had thought it was welcome, I might have done that. I had begun to have health issues, and my doctor had suggested that the stress was to blame. He told me just to let go of the whole thing. My eczema cleared up when the strike was over. He had been right!

I finished that semester, and I was transferred for September to New Toronto High School. I have no doubt that my strike behavior caused that change. Many of the staff were very gracious at the time of my leaving, recognizing that I had had the right to do what I did. It had been a good two and a half years, and I did keep in touch with a couple of those teachers for years. Again, I obviously learned a great deal about my teaching, colleagues, and about myself. Yes, in that school I certainly did change. Whether or not it was my choice, I was following the wisdom of Professor Love; I was in for new experiences more than I realized!

Chapter 11

New Town Secondary School (NTSS) (1978–June 1988)

I f you have ever started a new job, you know about being nervous. My classes in this new school included teaching English at all different levels. The class that worried me the most was a group of students who had been socially promoted to high school from the elementary system. Those students were known to be ill equipped to handle even the lowest level of grade 9 English work. In a regular class, they were bored and frustrated and caused many problems. The wonderful solution was to put them all in one room!

The other scary idea was that I had been told by the teachers in the last school that I would have to be really strict here. They had heard horror stories of the behavior at NTSS. I believed maybe the stories were true after seeing that the town water tower behind the school. It had the huge sign hand-painted on it: "NTSS SPXXXX Team!" Obviously, that had been done by the brave local heroes.

Before starting to work there, I drove around the area to see where the students lived. There were some very expensive properties right on the lake, a few low-rise apartments, and a lot of little well-kept houses. They had been the cottages for the rich people from the city of Toronto in the old days. That area was approximately one decent buggy ride from downtown. Those days the water had not been polluted, so the lovely beaches there really meant cooler summer holidays. In my first years of teaching here many factories were still in operation. Generally, it was considered a working class area.

The change to this new school environment was obvious to me when meeting my English classes. They were not as scary as predicted but maybe because I was being so scary! One of the first writing assignments I had given them was to do descriptions of their bedrooms. I stressed the importance of using all the senses. I would remind them, "Be sure to mention different sensory perceptions when doing a description: for example, mention the sights and also smells and sounds." Thus, in their writing, there were the usual things like clothes on the floor but different ideas too. Here, I read about the regular hum of the factory machinery next door, the smell of the rubber from the manufacturing of tires at the Goodyear plant, and the voices of the people fighting next door.

Another major difference was in the lower economic status of the students' families. One attractive petite girl from the grade 11 class suddenly did not come to class at all; yet she had been attending regularly. Upon my enquiring about her absence, I learned she had had to leave school to go to work. The story was that she had been driving her brother's car when she was drunk and had had a bad accident. He had said she had to work to earn money to pay him back. Had she been hurt? Would she ever come back to school? She did not! Whatever happened to her? This reality was hard for me to accept. I knew that in the last school more than one father had bailed a boy out of a similar situation. It was a big lesson for me. Money does make life easier! Would

Alice not have had a better life if there had been more money to rescue her?

One boy later told me about what used to happen when he was in grade 8. If his mother were on the day shift, he would bring his friends to his house for a liquid lunch. The ones who could still walk would return to school. They had never been caught! That was one of the boys who talked with me a lot, and I knew him well. Later, I even went to his home to drag him out of the house to go to school to take an exam. It was needed to complete his credits so he could graduate. He did! Did the parents have any interest? What was more important, the job or the child's graduation? I was learning! A job was, and hence money, really was a necessity for survival.

The parent-teacher nights were also different. At the last school, I had even had to defend myself when a mother accused me of being too harsh when I took spelling marks off a student's good English exam. The father, a teacher, had backed me up in that case. At NTSS, I soon learned to first talk to the student when there was an academic problem. Later I would call home, but only if I got the impression that there might be a helpful response. If I learned that mother or both parents, were out of the picture or were drunk, then the problem was mine. Maybe, I failed. Later I met a teacher who had handled a similar problem differently. He would buy a case of beer and go and knock on the door to try to get the parent interested in the value of his/her child's education. My hero! We had one outstanding, wonderful vice principal, who also made a lot of home visits. I did some such visiting toward the end of my stay at NTSS but only with the permission of the involved student.

The parents who did come to talk to teachers were genuinely caring. They were fully aware of the value of education and of their child's progress. One lady dropped in on her way to the night shift. She had curlers still in her hair and my Maritime accent. We immediately recognized our similar backgrounds and were comfortable with each other. I had found my niche as a teacher. Needless to say, her girl was doing well in school. Another caring lady I also came to know well. Her son was in both of my grades 11 and 12 English classes. She and I became best of friends. She was the type to organize huge community gatherings when she was well enough. Later, I came to know her even better as she helped me with problems of my own. I spoke at her funeral. As in other schools, I believe it is parental interest that is the best motivator for student success.

Many of the homes I had seen and later visited were filled with people from the Maritime Provinces. They, like me, missed the ocean, and the big lake was the next best thing. If they had come with some education, it was often not up to the standards expected in Ontario. (Does that not sound familiar?) It was particularly noticeable if they had come from the Newfoundland outports. In some cases the need was such that they were placed in my grade 9 classes for special students. At NTSS I came to love these groups as the number of students was then kept under fifteen, and so I could really help them.

I had one Newfoundland girl who was eager, friendly, and loved to tell stories. She made great headway in writing, especially if I let her do her own thing. She wrote very long stories without periods but interesting! She did catch on to our way but slowly! When I had asked if she liked Toronto, her reply was "Oh yes, miss. Here I babysits and I gets my own money. I even gots my haircut this week in a real beauty parlor." That plural "s" in the first person singular was totally acceptable in Shakespeare's England and in the Newfoundland outports where, until recently, people were still using that archaic language. I met these people of the older generation when visiting there. Will they ever change? I hope not! It is charming. My sister lived quite a few years in Newfoundland, and I have caught her saying words such as "maids" for girls and "byes" for boys.

Each September, the policy of social promotion from elementary school resulted in many nearly illiterate students joining my grade 9 English special group. One of the girls from the countryside in Jamaica had sat under the trees, and her reading lessons were only from the King James Bible. In these cases, it was often all teachers had to work with. There were other students from these isolated locations who actually did have more skills. Another Newfoundland student told me of the harrowing drive to Ontario. He and his family had had to go through Quebec. Their old car had given trouble, and they could not communicate with the mechanics in either French or English! I asked how they were surviving here, and he said that his older brother, who was seventeen, worked at delivering milk. When I asked if the brother could read and do the required arithmetic, the answer was "Oh no, miss, I does it for him every night." I guess he himself was learning fast; so was I!

This school became home to me. It was in my comfortable rut! I also was learning another valuable life lesson: if one is to be successful, to have a fulfilled life, one can find something to love in all people we meet. I look back now at a little boy who had been in a one of my much earlier school classes. His name was George, and I thought of him as a proper monster. I had treated him that way. I expect he thought of me as a monster too! I had sworn that I would never like any man named George. Fortunately, I now know and love a couple of wonderful Georges who are very important in my life. Slowly, my attitude had changed. My job had become easier. I looked forward to going to work. As this new pope has just said, "Who am I to judge?" At NTSS, this new attitude was applied to the boy whom I insisted must continue to sit where I could watch him. I had seen him cheating once. We both knew I had watched him write down an answer after checking the paper of the girl across the aisle. Also, I found it hard to scold any student who had tickled my fancy even if he/she had done something amusing that was slightly against the rules. I could not help but smile when I was pontificating, and a boy who sat right under my nose would cheekily whisper, "That is a crock, lady!" Sometimes one has to stop and just enjoy the humor.

The teaching became easier as the students became accustomed to the idea that I would be sitting in the open-door classroom after school and marking their work. They would drift in to talk. Usually it was to tell me of recent happenings and of their achievements. Occasionally, it was about a problem. It might even be for an interview I had requested. One boy dropped in frequently, and finally we discussed his choice of courses for that current year. Hence, I discovered that he was taking the grade 9 typing course for the third time. He had regarded it as an easy credit, and the guidance office had accepted it as a second credit when he had taken it twice! He just thought, why not do it again! These sessions were times for problems to surface and where they felt free to talk. Basically, they wanted a willing ear. It became known that I was an adult who would listen and neither judge nor gossip later. As in the previous school, it was at these times that I was shocked to hear about their risqué social lives. I was surprised as I knew they had little money to throw around. I heard about the ways one can illegally freely attend the famous rock concerts and about what happened there. Once in a while, however, there really was a desperate crisis that needed to be talked through.

Once, a grade 12 boy rushed in crying, slamming the door shut, and announcing, "I'm going to kill myself tonight." I just grabbed him and hugged and hugged him until he was calm enough to talk. We did not even open the door for a while. In today's teaching climate, where a teacher is never, never to touch even a small child with a bleeding wound, I would probably have been fired! I am a mother. It was obvious that this child needed that hugging. I like to think that I would still do it today. The problem was a broken heart, which was and still is the bane of the lives of high school students. It happened often enough to me! Most of us survived high school, as did that young man. It did help to have my ear. It is often all that is needed.

I could occasionally be asked to break rules. "Miss, would you please cover for me as I will be away tomorrow? There is no honest note I can write a note for my absence." This really meant "I need to talk." Of course it was, as by this time, a given that they all wrote their own notes, whether or not they were sixteen! I would ask what was up, and all I had to do was not report the student as being away for my class. It was usually a very important matter to them. One girl explained that she had only one pair of jeans. She could not come to school because the next day would be her only chance to wash and dry them. I knew her circumstances. I knew it was true, and those jeans were probably her only attire. Another case of needing a note was even more moving. The young man told me that his girlfriend was pregnant, and he wanted to go with her when she had an abortion. That involved a long talk. In the end I told him I was proud of him for helping her as most women seemed to go through that agony alone. As it turned out, they did not get married. They were very young.

A couple of years later, this same young man called one night to ask if I would be home because he wanted to come to show me something. He knew that I liked old-fashioned cars, and he and his buddy came to my home to show me a Model A Ford that he had restored. I was able to tell them of my memory of a ride in such a rumble seat when I was just three or four years old. I considered myself well thanked!

Other circumstances where I broke the standing rules usually involved the grade 9 classes. There I was dealing with pupils with emotional, social, or reading problems. There was one incident when a frustrated boy threw a desk across the room. He did not intend to hit anyone; it was just his way of dealing with his intense feelings. I was relieved when one of the older, bigger, more mature boys just gave me a hug and said, "Don't worry, miss. I'll just take him out and we'll go for a walk." They came back later. In the meantime, the rest of the class just carried on as if it had not happened.

I later discussed this with the principal who agreed with my action, but we decided to have the parents in for a talk. I knew that the child was spending his nights sleeping in an abandoned moving truck. He told me that was not too bad as the movers had left the mats that he could use for blankets. After explaining our concerns, we asked the mother and sister if their doctor could be consulted. He was. Later, we found out that the doctor thought there was nothing wrong! It ended with my experiencing the frustration! There was no help for the child. Is he now one of our street people? Maybe he is in jail where he at least will be fed and warm? Alice certainly did not consider that a perfect solution!

T. L. C.

Another explosion of frustration ended better. An older, larger boy in the front seat had failed his exam, and there was no amount of fixing the mark that I could do. When I passed it back to him, he just made it into a ball, fired it at me, and said, "F——k you!" The rest of the students gasped when I said, "I'd feel the same if I were you. I'd suggest you just go for a walk to cool off. We'll talk later." He did. We did. He really could not read very much. As we talked, he said he thought that he would be able to get a job with an uncle. I said, "Go, with my blessing." He was basically a fine person, and the person who hired him would have a good worker. He had tried to the best of his ability in that class. Whatever happened later?

There were also the pupils who did not talk with me much to me until after they had left my classes, maybe years later. For one boy it was even after his high school graduation. This young man had given me a beautiful model car he had built. He knew I thought he was a good student in English, but we had never really talked. When he had his own apartment, he wanted my approval. Then we came to know each other well, and I learned about his life in Africa. The solid British background explained his superior use of the English language! His parents had been and still were missionaries. Later, I went with his parents, who were home on a sabbatical, to attend his graduation from college in aircraft maintenance. His hobby became helping to repair antique airplanes at that club in Hamilton. I sometimes wonder if he still does it. We have met since by accident in a store, and he proudly told me he has a family with two beautiful daughters.

There were others of these "friends later" students. One girl whom I knew well asked me to speak at her wedding. She had other guests from that same class and I had a lot of fun dancing with the old boys who were now so all grown-up! Another girl was a voracious reader; I visited at her place of work, a bookstore, where she has been a great success. There were many such cases, but one really stands out. Many years later, when I was working with Alice, I was to be presented with the *Sun* newspaper award for Teacher of the Year. This young man and his wife both took time off work to attend the ceremony. He gave the very flattering, much-appreciated speech. Guess who had written the letter of recommendation saying that I should receive the *Sun* newspaper award? That was an easy question. Yes, Alice did. Because of her background, she fully understood what I was achieving in that classroom.

It was time for a bit of a break. I needed to increase my qualifications to be able to have higher pay. I, therefore, worked one year when I taught only in the mornings. That gave me the time to go to U of T and to finish the two needed courses to be able to take the English specialist certification. Also, I audited lectures by the famous professor Northrop Frye. I got those necessary credits but learned more from him! In fact, his ideas changed my life and my ideas of God. A couple of times, I brought students down with me to experience a university campus and a lecture. I thought I was encouraging them to have further education. My other professors were most helpful and accommodating.

These students were from the grade 12 English classes. Thankfully, when I was in my second year at NTSS, I was able to balance the number of those English classes with some classes in family studies. That involved my taking summer courses to get the piece of paper that said I was qualified! Was I? I know I loved doing it, but probably the real professionals with the proper degrees just shook their heads as I asked my dumb questions. I worked with some wonderful women who taught me a great deal. One lady was a fashion graduate from Ryerson's excellent program, and she even allowed me to use her college notes. Those relaxed classes were the most fun I ever had in teaching. It involved mainly sewing, and classes were usually relatively small. It was not uncommon to have fifteen girls and one or more boys. Once, using my newfound knowledge, the students designed dresses for themselves. They made their patterns and sewed the garments. We then had a fashion show. The class's favorite, our one boy, made a spectacular T-shirt.

There were also some cooking classes similar to what I had often done before. There, we occasionally had our vice principal in for a taste test of our muffins. The classes loved his visit as he was very much a people person and a favorite with students. He, like me, was in the right school. One time, a grade 12 class was small enough that we were able to plan for an entire nutritious meal. I do not remember who paid for the food, but for that class, we went to my home for the day. The cooking was done there and we had a proper dinner party. It was another learning experience that was also fun.

The trend in family studies changed gradually during this time. It had been "cooken'" and "sewen'" in the first years. By the time I had my last classes, the stress was on social issues. I honestly believe that there should be stress on both fields of study for survival! Just consider today how few marriages there are and how few of those last. What will the many future bachelors live on?

In one section of the social living program, I had to instruct in types and dangers of sexual diseases. Today, that would be done in the earlier school years or in the physical education classes. I had one older woman who had come from Newfoundland and who had already had a child. This particular incident happened the day the inspector had come to see me teach to approve my special family studies qualifications. We were to discus AIDS. My friend the librarian had me all prepared with the latest information; I was ready for class but not ready for my Maritime friend. She asked him what he was doing in this class. He said he was there to see Miss Douglass teach. She then told him, "I don't know why you need to do that. She is the best teacher in the school."

In my opinion, the best such course that our board instituted was family living. We had semesters with long ninety-minute classes and a half year for this course. In one version of this, we started with the sexually transmitted diseases and how to choose a life partner. Then we progressed to planning a pretend wedding, and we actually staged one. A divorce lawyer came in to explain what a legal union entailed and the importance of a marriage contract. This exercise was possible as each class was to have equal numbers of girls and boys. The students loved it all. We finished the course with information about birth control and discussions about the raising of children. The whole course was the most useful I ever taught. It was offered only four years and wrongly abandoned. Had there been complaints about the birth control aspect? We had had a lot of enjoyment and honest exchanges of knowledge. The relative informality meant that I came to know those pupils well. It was comfortable enough that they all felt free to ask what they really did need to know. I would stress here particularly the work we did with financial budgeting. Generally, it is never done in school and is so necessity for successful marriages.

As in the former school, my contribution to the extracurricular staff activities at this school was the setting up and execution of an awards program. We collected each student's points for academic excellence, extra contributions to school life, and all team participations. The record keeping without a computer was horrendous! At the June assembly, the school honors were presented, and I was the master of ceremony, having ordered the trophies, badges, and certificates. The helpful librarian collected the students' points. I believed in the value of this program. It has since become even more significant. Most universities now require proof of the fact that the applicant is an all-around person.

I cannot even remember doing the awards in 1980–1981. Maybe I did not! That was the year I was the staff advisor on the yearbook called the Neutron. Was I financially responsible? I thought so. My family members were busy with their own lives, so not knowing what was involved, I had volunteered when asked. I had believed that I had time to work with the motley student crew that had been assembled to produce that yearbook. The pictures in the book indicated that many had signed up to work, yet predictably, as the time came to assemble it, there were the faithful few! We even met a couple of times in my basement; there were layout sheets spread on the washer and the dryer. Those who came worked hard, and we had fun. The project manager was a boy who was registered in grade 13 but rarely went to class. One boy, who was supposed to be in my own English class, I saw only at these work sessions. Later he had to do the credit at summer school. He told me it was easier! Remember, being over sixteen meant the student made up his own mind about attendance!

I remember others as equally diligent in the service of the book but who were often not attending school too regularly. However, only one person asked for his book money to be returned; the student project manager had had his picture in it too often! I did not blame that boy! It was the habit for the teachers and students to sign each other's yearbooks. I see that one of the boys who had helped had understood the agony I had endured. He signed my copy by writing, "Miss Douglas's book, blood, sweat, tears, time, anger, and final relief." Those students and I became very close and they called me Mom. A couple of them still do. Most of the work sessions were held at an assigned room in the school, and some sessions were in the evenings.

I learned a lot and I changed a lot. I knew for sure that I never again would be yearbook advisor. There were tangible rewards beyond just a good book. I liked the kids, and couple of them at age fifty are still in contact, one frequently. I became involved in their lives, and for a few, maybe I was even a positive influence. In teaching that is not something one usually knows for sure.

I did know many other students well. They had just wanted to have an adult who would listen uncritically. I visited a couple in the psychiatric sections in hospitals, went to parents' funerals, held them through heartbreaks. Of course, there were times I was let down and disappointed with their behavior. I did let them know! One of the best exercises that I thunk up for one grade 12 group was giving each one a novel from my own collection. I suited the book to the reading level and needs of each person. They then were required to do an oral book review and read some selections of their book to the class. That backfired a bit when one of the more mature girls had a Margaret Lawrence novel and she chose to read a sexy scene. The audience gasped, and then we all had a good laugh. It was all I could have done! The following is about the boy who had *The Picture of Dorian Grey* as his novel—guess why!

He gave us all a good laugh one day. He had been too smart for his own good and had been caught out on the roof of the first story of the school. Our room was on the second level as were several others. He had climbed up thinking he would cause a humorous distraction by coming into the class through the window. Most of the other second-story teachers, sensing his predicament, had locked their windows, as did we. When he finally arrived, we were all in stitches. They could hardly wait to describe the entire incident to me. Life as a teacher is just so much easier when one lets it all flow naturally, if possible.

Another incident that involved that class was the bright idea of a boy from Argentina. He had been sent to Canada to avoid having to fight in their war with England. His mother had met me and suggested she would like him to learn a bit of English. He did, but quite a bit of the vocabulary was not from my class! He was a party animal with money, and he taught the others how to have fun after hours! This incident happened on my last day before my planned year off. Most of the students had come just to say their good-byes so we could do the usual promises to keep in touch. Then he walked in with a roll of the sod that was being laid on the football field. He announced that he was contributing to the party by bringing lots of grass! All we got was a laugh, not high!

I can think of another student joke that was fun. One morning my students for the special grade 9 class had all arrived early by prearrangement. Boys will be boys; there were usually very few girls in those classes! They had made a big noise and a couple of other teachers had checked but not interfered. They had warned me, however, as I approached. They had turned the seats to face the back of the room, including my own desk. We all had a great laugh and they had a wonderful time explaining how it was done and when. I taught the class standing backward! We changed it in the last few minutes. The boy with the idea was one of the students whom I later visited in a psychiatric hospital ward. He told me he had come from Eastern Europe. The most significant incident in his life to date was his mother had reported he was born in the back of a Volkswagen Beetle! The things on learns if one listens!

Yes, I really enjoyed myself when I was teaching at NTSS, and thankfully the administration appreciated what I was doing and why. One of the principals told me at lunch one day that it was such a pleasure to come down the hall where I was working and to hear the whole class laughing, the teacher included. I was blessed! Yes, however, I was ready for the next year's planned break. I knew that I was too close to the students and cared too much. We all needed a rest from each other, and my throat needed a rest. Really, I guess I had talked too much. Had I not listened as much as I thought I had?

Chapter 12

My Paid Year Off

C hapters 11 and 13 tell of my doing what my Professor Love had warned me not to do: I had spent those years teaching basically the same things in the same place. Was that a smart move? You be the judge!

This break was for the entire school year 1988–1989. Our Board of Education and Teachers Federation jointly agreed to a plan for all staff called "four over five." Many boards had accepted such plans because there were unemployed teachers, new teachers who are getting neither experience nor jobs. It meant that I could work for four years for 80 percent of my salary and be off for one year, and I would still have the same 80 percent salary. The timing of the years had to be agreed upon by both the board and the teacher. There was a small cost to the board as I received my benefits for all five years. They were saving, however, by hiring new teachers at much lower salaries. I have heard there are other variations of this scheme now.

Gratefully, I embraced this opportunity because I was truly burned out physically, mentally, and emotionally. There were at least six and a half years left for me to teach; it looked like an eternity. I really did love my job, and the students . . . probably too much. My body was also complaining. Getting too old too fast was no fun. I truly planned to be a new, changed person when I returned next fall. The first thing, therefore, was to assess my situation. Where was I headed? My husband at this time was busy being successful and doing a lot of traveling. He was feeling useful and was enjoying himself, and I was working! I looked around and decided first I wanted a house with more light. I wanted to learn more but by taking courses with exams! Next, I looked into the mirror and saw an old woman. Obviously, I also wanted more fun in my life. I tackled my concerns with a vengeance.

The first on the wish list had to add to the house so that it would be completed while I was still at home. That change meant more windows and more closet space. Concerning more courses for pleasure, I discovered that the women who did not work spent their time doing these just for fun. That was a novel idea for a teacher! I did three art classes. That teacher said to us, "One person here has real talent. The rest of you can learn to draw." I did so learn but also learned what it felt like to be put down by a teacher—not good!

Another course I took was fun too, and there I was overly proud of my accomplishments. It was the "ladies learn to ski" class at Mount Saint Louis. It was very hard for me. Finally, I made a turn without falling; the ladies all loudly cheered, "Yeah, Barb!" I have since found out that what I suffer from is called dyspraxia. Then I just thought I was stupid or spastic. Those skiing lessons were a great learning experience for a teacher. The skiing teacher had been so patient, not like the art teacher!

Each time I looked into the mirror I could see the effects of all the stress and my double chin. I complained to my doctor who referred me to a plastic surgeon. The suggestions that doctor made encouraged me, and in the spring I saw the results. It was the best present I could ever have given myself. It was day surgery.

One of the young men whom I had befriended came to pick me up because my husband was working when it was to leave the hospital. The nurse told my former student to help his mother get dressed; we had great giggles. He said, "I'm much better at taking this stuff off!"

Now, here's the really fun part of that year. We were able to take trips to San Francisco and to Germany. Our daughter was studying that year at Freiburg University. The summer of 1989 was busy with visiting relatives and preparing for next year at what was to be a new school in our old building.

I had had a teacher inspection before that year off. The man had come in to see what I had been doing with my special grade 9 classes. He had looked thoroughly at their workbooks. Afterward, he told me that I was not to try to be checking everything they wrote. How else could they learn? My marking was not only to make the corrections, but I needed to let them know I cared that they did the work correctly. I refused to change! In jail later, inmates used to ask me why I cared. They had never had that problem before. This was one area where Alice had been such a help in jail as she too cared about the students.

When school started in September, there was an added student population from a nearby school. I hoped my reputation had preceded me. Life would be okay if my voice and feet did not give out. I was counting on my newly minted self-image and my newly minted orthopedic supports!

Chapter 13

Brooks Collegiate Institute (BCI) (1989–1990)

Another new school? No! The name was new, the decorations were new, a few paint jobs were new, half of the student population was new, many of the staff were new—I was not! This area of Toronto was doing what is referred to as maturing. It had become obvious to the Etobicoke Board of Education that it would be more financially viable to put the two school populations into one building and to rent out the empty one. Hence, it would not be politically correct to cause the others to move into our old school if it kept the old name, so our old school all became the new one! Returning to our school was, for me, a new experience. It had been reborn. I am sure that for the staff and pupils from the old Alderwood High School it was traumatizing. It would be especially so for the students who had spent the earlier years of their high school education in their home area. They all now had longer walks to get to Lakeshore. The place did indeed come alive with the greater number of bodies around.

I was aware of it in the smoky staff room. Throughout the building, the old, cozy, close atmosphere no longer was prevalent. We gained some good bridge players from the new staff. We, as members of the older staff, had again to establish our reputations as control freaks who were kind! I have made this a new chapter because it really was just the same as starting again in a new school. I was still teaching the family studies; some of those stories are ones I have already recounted. In these classes things did not change; we all had fun, and again behavior was never really a problem.

The English classes were, however, different. They were larger and noticeably so in the grade 9 special classes. I saw more problems that were related to the system of refusing to fail the students in the elementary grades and passing students on to the high school based only on their size and age. Some of the boys really could not read. In one case, when I phoned the mother, I was told that I was the first teacher to contact her with that news. Tragically, it appeared that she might be telling the truth.

In the upper grades, I had previously been aware of students who were high in class. It was usually marijuana they were using, so as they were just smiley and placid. I would wait until later to make them aware of the fact that it was a useless to attend the class; their presence was their business as they were over sixteen. In the LCI grade 9 classes, I now had couple who were either so drunk or so high, they were falling out of their seats. I usually followed up with phone calls to parents and later with conferences involving the administrators, parents, and myself. In one case, we again suggested the boy be referred to the family doctor. As mentioned before, that was, as usual, a useless exercise. Another case was one in which I got what I had expected to be the answer, so I followed my old practice of talking first to the pupil. He told me his story when I questioned him at the end of the day when he was more sober. His mother had died recently, and his father provided the liquor as he himself was an alcoholic. He had no older siblings who might have helped. I just said that he was welcome to come to class, whatever the condition, but he was to sit at the back, and that I hoped he would come often after school. He did.

That boy never did complete his year. Another alcoholic rewarded my concern by placing his broken whiskey bottle behind the front tire of my car. Fortunately, I had found it! What a loud cry for help that was! Again, we had already gone through the route of school conferences and the refusal of the family doctor to make any further referrals.

A third alcohol problem was in a regular grade 9 classes, and his friends had come to ask for my help. He drank heavily but only after school, not in class. In fact, it was one of the local school drug dealers who asked me to help him! In that way, it was the same family-type atmosphere as it had been in old one. The students looked out for and cared for each other. That dealer sold pot from the pockets of his heavy overcoat, a coat he wore no matter what the temperature! The increase in the student population meant a major increase in the drug selling and use. It became no different from our other large high schools. A teenage girl I knew well who attended a different large school had her locker next to that school's "drugstore." The dealer's uncle in Jamaica mailed him a shoe box full of pot each week; he did a brisk Friday business. This seemed to reinforce the perception that was prevalent then and being embraced by more people now: alcohol is a far worse problem than drugs.

The boy with the weekend drinking problem was from a Maritime family, so I had the old familiar connections. He had been his mother's support and caregiver until she had recently died at a young age from breast cancer. I came to know the father and older brothers quite well. An uncle was also involved in getting him into AAA. Later in the summer, I really became involved when the hospital called for me to come to visit him. He had asked for that call to be made. This involved his first suicide attempt. He had gone under a moving GO train and had lived! We were together a lot after that, and sometimes he came to school. I knitted, to his specifications, a black sweater. Later, he inherited money and went to live in Vancouver. I received a couple of wonderful letters. I have saved them as his writing and designs are so creative. There was no word for years after that. Then, out of the blue, he phoned one evening. He had found a place to live. It would appear he is one of the men that are being helped by their new program in the lower east side of Vancouver. If he would only phone or write again!

Here I will digress as I have the greatest sympathy for our present city mayor. He has been raked over the coals by the press because he made the mistake of being too close to and obviously even photographed with his buddies. It appears he tried to help those boys when he was their football coach. Unfortunately, he became too caught up in their culture. At this time in my career, I was really too involved in the lives of some of my students. There were no cell phones to picture me with my friends. Yet any adult who is seriously talking to them, questioning their ideas, and actually listening and trying to help can be a subject of criticism. In spite of it all, I believe that our mayor has probably been an influence for good in many of their young lives.

Obviously, my reputation was again established as a person who would listen and who could be trusted to keep quiet and to offer help if it was at all possible. Lots of this talking and listening continued after school, even in the evenings by phone or in occasional home visits. I remember one big boy from the special grade 9 class who had left school. He had managed to get a job on a garbage truck. He returned one afternoon to assure me that I was not the reason he had left. He wanted to assure me he was happy and to show me the "new" leather jacket that he had found when doing his new job!

As you can see, when necessary, problems were referred to the office but only if I thought it would help. The new vice principal had, however, a reputation of being on the side of the student, not the teacher. This made me leery. He was reported to have told one miscreant to just go back to class and be quiet. His exact words were quoted more than once in the staff room: "Be good.

She is probably on her period!" We knew about that because the secretarial staff was on our side.

Once, I broke up a fight between two girls. It was over a boy, of course! I just took the knife away from the one who was in my classroom and sent the other back to her class. I was stronger and had not been worried about being hurt. The knife went into my purse, and I delivered it, with the story, to the office afterward. I never gave the names. The principal and I agreed that the girls were scared enough, and he agreed with my handling of the situation. The owner of the knife did not get her property back! It stayed in the office.

That was not the only knife I saw. The next one I did not remove; that was held by a big boy who came to visit me when he was out on parole and was celebrating his freedom by being drunk. I knew we had had a good relationship, but I was scared. He sat quietly after I gave him a seat at the back, and he took out his knife to carve his name. Later he told me he came to see me because he felt safe there! That year I had been assigned to remote classroom. Then my reputation of having good class control was well tested. I was down near the technician's office, and my room had easy access from the street. The office buzzer in that room did not work. Anyone could just open the outside door, go up the stairs, and enter. Here, one grade 9 English class was a particular challenge. One girl would announce her late arrival with loud music on her boom box. To have sent her to the office would have meant another similar arrival about twenty minutes later. Two girls would arrive drunk after lunch, having made money in their lunch hour! There were the usual immature boys who thought that everything that happened was a cause for hilarity and for misbehavior. Talk about teacher stress! Years afterward, I met one of those good students from that class. She was working at the *Sun* newspaper and we discussed that horrible situation. People used to ask me if I felt scared in jail! No way, I was safer there!

Knives were obviously the weapons of choice in those times. There was one interesting occasion, however, with the grade 9 special class. I had asked, as usual, if anyone knew where the missing person was and if he would be likely to be present today. The students all laughed, and one said, "Oh no, miss, he was picked up yesterday with his brothers when the cops did a roundup of the local coke gang." When he returned a few days later, being on probation, I had to ask to make sure that he was not still carrying the pistol! The others had told me he had usually carried one and had shown it to them. He assured me that he would never have used it in my room and that it was really only a starter's pistol! How do teachers stand the tension today when guns being so prevalent?

Again, teaching the family living, a new format, of course, was a joy. These classes were safer and fun and such a relief from the English marking. In that family living course, there were a couple of sections that were particularly enjoyable. For one, we had to take a look at family life in pioneer Canada. This allowed me to organize a bus trip to Pioneer Village, one of my favorite places. These students had never been there. One school in our school board had taken younger pupils there for an entire week. How unfair! I am old enough to have lived in a home without plumbing and used a wood-burning fire for heat. On that particular trip, the guides were good, the weather was sunny, and we got some great pictures. The students were truly all eyes and ears. It was a totally new experience for them to see living history. I filled in any gaps. I was asked, "Miss, did you do that when you were little in the olden days?"

When we returned to class the next day, they were each to write a weekly diary based on the premise that they each were a parent in those olden times. They were to tell about the work of each day. I reminded them that there was no birth control, and so there were a lot of children running around underfoot to be clothed and feed. The diary should include church, or a barn dance, or a sewing bee, or a barn-raising bee. The class was also to learn about the amusements and crafts of those days, and I had them trying rug hooking or making rag dolls or some other toys. At the end of the semester, we paid a visit to donate our gifts to the place where local people now go for social help (LAMP). Since it was near where most of them lived, they themselves could go, should they or their relatives need such help. The students were surprised by the number of senior citizens who were there for a foot clinic. The guide told of all their available services. This family living course was one that was stopped to save money. What false economy!

I was also allowed to accompany students on other trips that involved fun learning. Are they also cancelled now? We then had an outdoor education program. One weekend, we took a group on a rock climbing outing at Milton. Staying overnight in tents meant a female chaperone was needed. I volunteered and had brought a homemade bean supper and chocolate cake. I had as much fun as the pupils. They climbed; I did not! The next day the beans were a source of many jokes. The boys in their tents complained that we girls had had so much fun that we had kept them awake.

Surely having fun while learning is not a sin! Such trips are no longer considered affordable within a school board's budget. I know there are also new time restrictions imposed by the new need to have all students graduate by the end of grade 12. We used to have a week of fall camping for one grade each year. It involved an enormous amount of effort on the part of the teaching staff, but everyone had fun and horrors! Many of the student population had never left the city. The bus ride north to the conservation area alone was an eye-opener. I was a chaperone once when there was a huge panic in a tent full of girls. They screamed and ran because they had seen an enormous spider inside. They cleared out, and heroine Barb went in! Bravely, I carried out a daddy longlegs bug. There is more than one way to gain the respect of the students!

The grade 12 physical education class used to have a section in which the students were exposed to activities that might be useful to them throughout their lives. It involved activities such as golf. Once I was asked to accompany them on a trip to Horseshoe Valley Resort for skiing lessons. My classes of "ladies learn to ski" were beginning to pay off. I went on this ski trip as so few female teachers knew how. While most students had group lessons with the regular instructors, those teachers who knew how enjoyed themselves on the slopes with the very few students who had learned before. Again, the students were amazed that their teacher knew more than English; she also knew how to have fun!

There was, however, one grade 11 general English class in which there was not much fun in September. The students soon realized I expected attendance and work. They had thought it would be very easy to pass general level grade 11 English; I had thought my job was to prepare them to take grade 12 English, so they would be ready for college. There was a slight difference in goals. I was set to mark a lot of written work; they were set not to do it! Since they were over sixteen, the age in which attendance was their own business, and many boys decided that that this class period was their time to have a cigarette break with their friends. This meant a smaller class with an improved, more positive atmosphere for the rest. Then, it was a productive experience. I was able really to know them and their problems.

One boy to whom I spoke about his absence was often away because his father was dying and he was needed at the hospital. He phoned me when his father was sent home to die. I baked a cake and went to his home to sit with him and to hold his hand for an evening. That was the custom in his culture. We had previously discussed the problem of his not passing as I gave a zero for incomplete work. He knew he would have to repeat the course and told me he understood. At the end of the course when I submitted my marks with several failures, the principal insisted he be given his pass! One day after I retired, and the grass was being cut at my home, I heard, "Hi, Miss Douglass." It was another one of the frequently missing boys. He had been away often because he had been doing movie work as an extra. He was glad to see me and told me of his world work travels and of his new son.

I did enjoy the academic grade 12 English classes, despite of all the markings. I understand that now there are computer programs on which one can check for plagiarisms. I was not that lucky. Fortunately, when that occurred, it usually resulted from their using Coles Notes, and I owned copies of all of those! Such misdemeanors were rewarded with a zero as were late papers. That was the reward they knew they would have after the due date. These older students had my phone number, and most could easily find out where I lived. Students are smarter than most people give them credit for, if it is in their own interest! I was a hard marker but free with advice after school. Later, jail proved to be different. There I was Barb, no last name and no personal information— even for Alice!

Since these classes were preparation for grade 13, and later for college and/or university, most were serious students. Regarding content to be covered, it was not very different from that described earlier. Speeches again were part of my program. Oral reports were part of my emphasis on learning from print as well as TV. There was supposed to be more emphasis on the research for essays and on group work. I guess it was a foretelling of the time when more students would have the freer access to the Internet, which they now do. At that time, it was difficult to do proper research even with our very helpful librarian. It was the old complaint about lack of material if one assigned a common topic.

In these grade 12 groups some good poetry was produced. Some boys even wrote their own sonnets after we had studied that form. Personally, that was something I would or could never have attempted. There were good class discussions, some about life lessons from Shakespeare. Should Hamlet have spent so much time and effort looking for proof of his uncle's guilt? Why did he not just kill the murderer? How are you going to make life and death decisions your life? I got into a bit of hot water when we had free expression of opinion about the paranormal. I had proved that I could make a student turn around to look at me when they all faced forward—done by standing at the back and concentrating mentally on just him. In *Wuthering Heights*, what or who did Kathy really hear doing that scratching at the window? I had realized I would enjoy teaching more mature people. I previously had thought of them as scary. To summarize, here are a few of the parting comments from my yearbook.

"You are a friend as well as teacher."

"The spelling! Guess where I fell down."

"I don't believe I'm gonna say this, but thanks for giving me homework."

"Thanks for the shoves once in a while."

"TO forget you, I cannot do, but to forget me it's up to you."

"I'm not much for English but I had a great time in your class."

"You made English more fun and exciting. I'm trying not to make any mistakes!"

"You gave homework on the weekend, but it was a good year, I passed!"

"Nobody can make Shakespeare interesting, but you came close."

"I had fun in your class. Now, I really like English."

Yes, the larger school population did make a huge difference. I particularly missed the closeness of the smaller staff and the fewer students, and I was ready for a change! My throat told me so!

Chapter 14

Ontario Detention Center (The West) (1991–1996)

Yes, indeed, I had a new job, a transfer within the Toronto Board of Education, except now I was in jail! Yes, indeed, I was safer! The correctional officers (COs) were so present and so appreciative of the teachers. This jail is really the Ontario Detention Center (the West). The Ontario Detention Center was a very special school. Inmate students ages eighteen to twenty-one were, as were all six hundred inmates, waiting for their days in court. They could have been accused of any type of crime, so this jail has to be a maximum security facility. Our training programs made teachers aware of the dangerous ideas that inmates can think of with so much spare time. They had been allowed to smoke in those days, so we saw weapons made of foil from packages and even others made of soap and plastic toothbrushes! Each day as we went to work we passed through double-sally port doors so that the guard on duty could check to make sure we had brought no contraband for our students.

It truly was the dream job for me. Physically, it was such an improvement, especially for my throat, feet, and back. We worked with each student individually by sitting beside him/her. We dealt with one at a time. Mentally I was challenged as I was required to help each student with whatever study course she or he needed or wanted. I even did elementary math! Emotionally the demands were much the same, but we dealt with each student on a much more restricted but personal basis. We were not allowed to maintain any contact with any inmate after he/she left the institution. The only way a further contact happened was when the person was arrested for a new crime and so was returned to the West. One returning girl, who had street smarts, replied when she was asked why she came back, "Oh, I had to get my teeth fixed." Classes were always full in the winter. The former inmates were wise enough to know how to get picked up when they needed help, such as food and shelter.

First, I will explain our physical setup. We really were very restricted. There were restrictions in space. Our own locked classroom was in a small old office space that had been set up as a kitchen with study tables. There were restrictions in the number of teachers because the ratio was one teacher to six students. There were two teachers for the girls' class. We each escorted our own six inmates down the stairs from the ranges (living quarters) to the classroom. There were restrictions to our having in class only those girls on the approved list. In the male young offenders' section, there were just six boys in the each room, and they were delivered to the teacher by the COs. These COs, in both situations, were just outside the windows. It helped that it was known that any incident meant removal from our programs. Education was regarded by inmates as a privilege. The class time for the girls was two hours, twice a day between their meal times. They were to eat on their ranges, the cell units.

This meant that I *had* to go home for lunch. This worked out well as my husband had just retired and he made my lunch. A second restriction for me was I was not to stay after school. My time was so restricted that I had to have time off. Then I continued working all summer! What a shame! I was required to put in the regular number of teaching days—180. Thus, my husband and I could and did have holidays in the winter! In retrospect, I guess it was all these restrictions that improved my life so much.

That was not the only gift for me. The real gift was that the clientele was so much pleasanter. I am not kidding. They were polite, appreciative, and generally easier to love. Yes, they had had problems, but that was such a small part of each person whom I came to know. Some inmates were with us a long time. This applies to both the male and female populations. Once, at a party, I met some of my ski buddies' close friends—Toronto policemen. They all wanted to warn me about the vicious nature of some of the women that they knew I would have in my locked classroom. They were genuinely worried about me. I tried to assure them that I was not a naive bleeding heart regarding those women. I was fully aware of their potential to do harm. I honestly was not that trusting. I would search for desirable character traits in each person—admirable traits such as courage and persistence, which I would try to encourage. I did understand that there were some for whom I was not a help. As for the teenage boys, I was very glad that there was usually more than one CO outside those windows. The women really were older and more mature.

Some of the girls were more philosophical than I would have been. One girl wrote a good poem about the horror of working the street in her short outfit in the winter. Her attitude to jail was "Well, anyway, here I am, fed and warm at taxpayers' expense!" It was the common response. For those of you who are fortunate enough not to be acquainted with our judicial and court systems, let me tell you. It is presently Canada's greatest disgrace. The poorer you are when arrested, the longer you will wait until you have your day in court. I frequently heard the inmates say the expression, "If you do the crime, you do the time." That was the philosophical mind-set if and when they were caught! This attitude helped in the old days when they were often allowed time served or double time for the days spent at the West. Now they do not get that break. Another way they looked at it was "Look at all the other things I did for which they did not catch me." Remember, there are, however, cases of truly falsely accused. These people are often poor. Their cases can be further delayed as they wait days to be able to see a free lawyer.

Inmates often experience such frustrations that the feelings boil over. Writers of newspaper stories express wonder that there are fights in jails! Some of the best poetry I ever saw during my entire career expressed these intense feelings. They have the required deep emotional experiences to be able to write it. There used to be an organization that would publish it. That group also used to arrange exhibits for the inmates' artwork. These outlets were so important, and then it all stopped. Why?

For subject teaching we used the course books from the Independent Learning Centre (ILC), but we were allowed to assess their work. Our school board granted the credits as it does for any regular school. Since family studies was officially okay, we were able to do cooking and sewing. Ontario Detention Center had eighteen teachers and one principal. There was even one student who completed her requirements for graduation while she was with us. We held her graduation ceremony in our classroom. Jail administrators could attend; her parents could not! Many inmates on serious charges stayed long enough to complete more credit courses. The credits could be used outside or another jail.

We teachers had professional development days. These excursions really were stimulating and relevant visits to surrounding jails. It was important as that was where our students would go or would come from. Most of the girls never were given more than the usual thirty-day sentence for communicating, so they never did more time than their thirty days. When they received longer sentences, they went to do that time at federal jails or provincial jails, depending on the length of time of their sentence. We teachers visited a couple of institutions out on Mclaughlin Road. One was for our younger females, our future female students! We met girls who still thought a life of crime was very exciting and profitable. No matter if they are sentenced or not, most women are now out at Milton. It is very difficult for their children to visit, and that was very important. That separation is wrong!

The best professional visit we had was at Kingston to see the scary old P4W (prison for women). The building was then over two hundred years old and was still in use. If a woman had been found guilty of murder, she might come to the West while she awaited a special parole hearing to have her sentence reduced. Women who killed husbands in self-defense used to get the full twenty-five years. I knew several of them. The wall around the special exercise yard was so low that when one infamous inmate was being held, the newspaper photographers were able to go there, look over that wall, and take pictures of her when she went for her daily walk.

This is where I met Alice for the first time. This is where she had spent her first fifteen years of her incarceration. This is where she had been chosen as the perfect, the most trusted guide to take the teachers around! She did that well and had done the job before. We even saw her private cell, which I believe she had earned by her cooperative behavior. Proudly displayed were her sewing projects, and the books she was reading. Who knew that she was to become such an important part of my life? The murderers were the most interesting inmates. I had accepted that, even if convicted, there was the possibility that they were as innocent as they often thought they were. I sympathized with those who had chosen survival over death; I would have done the same. If your raging, drunken husband is threatening to shoot you or use a knife, do you stand idle or do you fight back? When these women came to the West, it was because they had been encouraged, after fifteen years, to appeal the length of their long sentences. For them, this place was also a welcome change. Often they acted as mothers, protectors, and advisors to the new girls.

Sometimes inmates helped us as teaches. One elementary teacher had been a big help too. Some of our girls needed the very basics in English and math. They often had missed a lot of school.

One girl had even been put out to work on the street by her mother at the age of eleven because her mother needed money for drugs. She claimed to have never really gone back to school after grade 3. Since we were teaching whatever was required by each pupil, I could find myself helping one girl with her English essay and then trying to explain the difference between 1/4 percent and 1/2 percent to the young girl who sold drugs!

It was the same "six pupils to one teacher" ratio when I was with the young offenders. Some boys could hardly speak understandable English. If one cannot speak English, it is hard to write it! Those classes needed stricter control and work on all aspects of English. After one quiet hour, I always made a break to work on the oral language. Then it was back to work as I gave each his assigned homework. They were seated at individual desks, in a circle facing out. I had a different six students in the afternoon. In each case, the class ended when they were taken back to their ranges.

I would start the conversation break, and each was called upon to express an opinion. At those breaks I honestly believe that I learned more than the boys did. I had read newspaper accounts of their culture; hearing it all firsthand was something else! I learned what it felt like to leave the loving grandmother who had raised you. Then you had to take a plane all by yourself to Toronto. The fear and the revulsion endured were palpable. How could a child love or have any respect for a woman who had abandoned her cute little baby? How can the abandoned boy love a "mother" who has another family with children, whom she has not left? Once I raised the topic of the common abandonment of children by fathers. Only one boy had actually known his father very well. The man had played in Bob Marley's band and he had taken his young son to the practices! Generally the father's disinterest was taken as a given. One time I raised the question of what kind of fathers they planned to be. I knew some had already fathered babies. One boy said he thought he would like to have forty babies. I asked, "Won't your wife get awfully tired?" There were great bursts of male laughter as he said, "Oh no, miss, forty baby mothers!"

My learning from our inmates happened in the women's class too, but there we had, instead, to encourage periods of silence. They were too articulate! General discussions about their common trades were forbidden. Those topics could lead to fights if, for example, one girl thought that the pimp had told her that she was number one wife, and she then found out that another girl had been told the same! Certain topics were just plain illegal, especially if the conversation might lead to methods of importing drugs. We did, however, have only one major fight incident. The principal had come in to talk with the teachers, so the lid was off and attention had been diverted. As the catfight erupted, each teacher grabbed and tightly held one combatant. We gradually separated them as we talked them down. They really had not wanted a ruckus; we knew that. The principal did not. He beat a hasty retreat—he had been scared! To those of us from the public system, it was nothing. However, we later discovered that the big blue panic button, in which we always had had such confidence, was disconnected!

Yet I was never worried in that room. The girls truly did not want trouble; they wanted to be there. After they left to go to their lunch, they were always checked to make sure nothing from the kitchen ever went upstairs to the ranges. Once, we had a wait at the window to be released. One girl showed me how she could use my car keys to open the door, and she did! I banged it shut again but was glad of the knowledge! The keys were the only personal thing I ever brought into the building.

You read right. We did have cutlery in that room, and we did have groceries, and we did cook. It was not for treats. It was for learning about nutritional values and for preparing meals that were cheap and good for their children. They were accustomed to having mainly fast food. I know that is a solution to a problem for many working mothers. Yes, most of the women were working mothers, and I was glad for them and for the sake of their children that we were able to do both cooking and sewing.

There was a sewing machine in this classroom. I also introduced crocheting and painting on cloth. That was as far a security policy would allow us to go. Such products they made were kept in the class and when completed placed into their property bags. I understand that they were allowed to continue the crocheting at P4W. The painting was used when they learned to sew by making a small cushion and then decorating it with the special paint before it was stuffed. Closing the opening meant learning hand-sewing. That could be useful for mending clothes. One of the girls teased me and said, "This will be really useful, Barb, when I'm sitting looking out the window and waiting for my drugs to be delivered!" The pregnant mothers were glad of the small afghan blankets that they could make for their babies.

No drugs and good food when one is expecting were frequent themes. Much later, when I was there volunteering, one of my former students saw me and joyously reported she was finally expecting a baby She said, "I remembered what you said, Barb. I stopped doing drugs as soon as I knew!" Oh dear, was that in the third month after much of the damage had been done? One girl who was expecting her fourth child used to crave calcium. We found that she had been eating our chalk! On another volunteering day, a former student told me about her new baby. She proudly said she had no new charges but had just asked to come back to clear up her old ones. In both cases, they seemed sincere.

My colleague who had lived as a bachelor told them about his easy and fast ideas for nutritious food. We made stews. The girls particularly liked his soup, which involved opening two cans, one of mushroom soup and one of tuna. It has better food value than have hamburgers and fries. We emphasized and served vegetables and fruit. The best meals of all were served on Christmas Eve. I cooked the turkey at home, and my husband came in with his good knife and carved and helped serve. The minister and the administrators were included as guests. The table was set up properly and we had minimal homemade decorations. I was allowed to buy, with my own money, a book for each girl. I knew them well enough that they were all different pocket books suited to their interest and reading levels.

We frequently received thank-you notes of appreciation from all the girls. Most were just for the warm, encouraging atmosphere and the help with their schoolwork. I include one here as it relates to the Christmas party this girl attended: "Dear Barb, Being here for Christmas last year turned out to be the best one I've had in a long time. It made me feel warm inside because each one of us girls received a different present. And we actually had a Christmas dinner that we all helped to make. I hope the girls next year have as good a time as I did. Thank you, Barb and Alphonse."

Many such thank-you notes are saved in my special scrapbook. They are all important to me, and if any of the girls ever see this book, I just want them to know. There were also a few letters that were sent to us after the girls went home. That was illegal! I know that receiving gifts certainly was illegal, yet we did! One very young girl who had been sent to Canada for her high school education had broken a law. During her ten months with us, she completed an English course and had a baby. Her thanks from Hong Kong was a parcel. It included candy for the girls, and that was most appreciated. Also much appreciated was the beautiful ivory necklace for me. I will treasure it for the rest of my life.

I hope you are beginning to understand why I say that this was the best job possible for me. There were other girls who stayed long enough for us to understand who they were and to love them. If I asked what the ones from other countries thought of Toronto, the reply often was "I don't know. I only saw the airport, the paddy wagon, and the inside of this jail!" There was one young pretty girl from California who was with us a long time long enough to complete her grade 12 English course. She and her friend had been picked up at the airport because there were drugs in the false bottoms of their suitcases. We heard about the great international trips they had had. It was not long before we knew of their being questioned in jail by the police. One girl was allowed to go home because she had broken down and told them all they wanted to know. Rats are not safe in jail. Was she then punished? Maybe!

Yes, rats, if not released, have to be in protective custody. There are also other little things you should know if you are ever incarcerated. Do not whistle. It conjures up the ghosts of all former inmates, and they might hurt you by giving you bad luck. Do not act smart or arrogant. Never annoy the range boss, the strongest inmate who has his/her power to control the range either through superior brains or superior physical strength. You do as he/she says, and you do it promptly! I think of one woman, who got all the food she desired by cupping, lowering the plastic glass from a height onto a head.

For a couple of summers we all learned about sex education. I was allowed to have a public health nurse come into the institution and to talk to us and answer questions. Was that ever necessary! Of course, it was now stopped! There were facts that were new to me, but I was also amazed by the ignorance of the girls who lived by the trade. Some did not even know what to look for in the way of evidence of sexually transmitted diseases, and their lack of birth control information was a shock. I even heard the comment "I can't get pregnant because I never have a climax!"

It became obvious that a big part of the power of the pimp was his manipulative skills. "He really loves me so well and I'm his number one wife!" That meant he had convinced her she was preferred above all the other "wives" in his stable. One young girl did say, however, that her attraction for her pimp was that he took her for rides in his cool new car. Honestly I did see that level of naivety and hunger for affection. We did not see the girls who are putting themselves through college by the trade. Obviously, these girls, like ours, had been raised in dubious circumstances by parents who had made them feel worthless, parents who had encouraged them to believe that they existed only to be used by men.

The saddest thing about the girls was the way they kept returning, especially if the charge were soliciting. I continued to see some of them even when I returned for volunteering after I had retired. There was no longer any education being offered for them. They were looking older and sicker and telling me as before, "Honest, Barb, this is the last time." I saw one who had been gorgeous when I first met her, and she had bragged about her special clients who were all doctors. When I saw her a few years later, she had a huge jagged knife cut across her left cheek. Obviously, she now had a violent, jealous pimp. You can understand why, although this teaching job was for me the best, it also was the hardest. I could do so little. Once, when I was discouraged, the minister who worked at the West counseled me by assuring me that I did do a little bit, she did do a little bit, and all the many compassionate correctional officers did do a little bit. Perhaps it did all add up to having at least saved some of them from death. We certainly had heard about the drug overdoses and about the violent deaths! One of my most encouraging things that happened took place when I was in the third year of being with the girls.

The *Sun* newspaper asks annually for nominations for teachers of the year. The pictures and write-ups are to be in the *Sun*. Each year they honor twelve teachers from the Ontario public school system. Alice, who had helped so much in the girls' room, had written the letter about what I was doing at this jail. She was still there. Later, we found out she had been refused her release by the parole board. There was all the rest of her time, ten years, to be spent at the P4W! What an enormous sadness we felt! Her boys had been so looking forward to having her with them. They were allowed to visit her at P4W for a short period. The irony is that the man who had supposedly done the deed was out after fifteen years! Later, I learned that one member of the Sun's selection committee did not think the public should know that the jail had good teachers. She had disapproved of my nomination. I was appalled! If even one inmate had never returned, I had saved taxpayers well over $100,000 a year

We twelve *Sun* teachers were all properly feted and even taken with our spouses to sit in the *Sun*'s box for a Blue Jays game. Before the game started, we met the Blue Jay players on the field, and we each were featured on the Jumbotron—my fifteen seconds of fame! What I really appreciated was a former student from New Toronto who gave a complimentary speech at the presentation ceremony. He and his wife had both left work to attend.

Administrators from the West attended, as did my coworker. Inmates did not!

My ego had been messaged by the love and confidences that the students at the West shared with me. The things I learned about their past lives made me understand completely why they had made poor decisions that led to their being in these unfortunate and humbling situations. I learned a lot about myself too, and I learned not to encourage self-pity either for myself or for any others who had confided in me. I tried to stress their youth and the hope for better and longer lives, for their future successes. The idea was "*You* are strong." What are *you* going to do to make sure that *you* cope better in future?

There were certainly days when I went home just shaking my head. How would I have coped if my mother had turned a blind eye to what her father or her husband was doing to me? How would I have coped if it was obvious that my mother had moved on and that my arrival in Canada was just a great inconvenience to her? How would I have coped if I had been forced to accept the knowledge that no one loved me, or even cared what happened to me? How would I have coped with numerous pregnancies by unknown fathers? How would I have coped with being rejected even by my pimp, the one person whom I had believed really "loved" me? I can only reflect on these situations and wonder what is happening to our girls now. The government, in its infinite wisdom, has now decided that younger inmates do not receive government sponsored help for education when they are enduring their long waits for their trials. Are there even enough government social workers for counseling; there were not enough when I was there!

I was just amazed and humbled by the perseverance and courage that I had seen in the face of such adversities. I could fully appreciate the solution of turning to the oblivion of alcohol and drugs. I had seen this in the high school, but usually some member of the family at least offered a measure of support. A grandmother or even an alcoholic parent was what those students at the West no longer had. One boy from the islands lived only to return and look after his grandmother who had loved him. He would do anything, and I mean anything, to get the money to go home to her. I could only listen, encourage, and hope to build up self-confidence to enable them to face their difficult futures. They just left. Yes, I worried about them, but there were no options left to do anything else. It was hard, even if it had been such a rewarding experience to be with these courageous people.

Did I ever break that new rule in education, the rule that says a teacher must never physically touch a student? You bet I did! I did, however, wait until I had been able to assess a person's mood and the body language. There were certainly some who were averse to any human touch because of the past experiences of beatings and abuse; with them, I would never have attempted even a light pat.

Many of my students could not trust anyone, but I felt that they could read in my eyes how much I cared. Tears and any welcoming gesture elicited hugs from me, and they were returned with gratitude. It was different with the boys. I was very careful not to give a touch, which might be misinterpreted. If there were a student who was not working in the study period of class, I would allow myself a light touch his shoulder or his hair. He would then look up, and I just had to give "the look" back to him, which said, "Get down to business." One boy asked in our talking recess why I did that. I replied, "Would you prefer that I yell at you?" They all answered, "Oh no, miss!" They had all been yelled at too much in their lives. I knew a touch was just as effective a tool!

I had learned what the most effective teaching tool is, if permitted by a student—it is a genuine love. It enables one to help them to help themselves. I left teaching knowing that I was tired, but I also knew I would miss my job very much. At the West, I had enjoyed talking to and being with more mature people. All the staff had been very friendly and helpful. Particularly so was the man teacher, the one who used to go to student homes with a case of beer. He was now teaching in jail too!

At the West, as indicated, the students were never to know anything about our personal lives. That was supposed to be for our own protection because inmates were assumed to be dangerous.

Again, I was not that naive! By watching out a window, the boys had figured which car I drove. They had then warned me that they found it very easy to steal things from that particular style of trunk. The supposed secrecy was not what kept me safe; it was the respect I had earned. I did miss the job after I left, but at seventy-seven I still teach when I get a chance. Watch out, if you are close to me; I may tell you how to do something or may impart some useless piece of information!

Chapter 15

Volunteer for Distance Learning at Local Jail

Since I had recently retired, my husband and I decided that we should start to enjoy the typical life of our retired friends. For another half year our school board continued the Etobicoke-Woodbine High School; then it was closed. The Catholic School Board was to take it over. Their bill, however, would be a lot smaller as they agreed only to take on the women's program. The men were left out, and the young offenders were moved to another facility. The new lady teacher from the Catholic Board of Education had the girls in the same classroom. She was allowed to offer only the regular Independent Learning Centre courses.

We traveled. As we loved to snorkel, we spent time in warm places, particularly in January. For a while there were bus trips. For seeing much of Alaska that was true; you have not lived until you have been to Chicken, Alaska! As our fridge magnet says,

"Millions of mosquitoes can't be wrong!" As we got older, we preferred cruising. It was a typical retirement until I could see that there was a place for me to do some volunteering at my old jail, the West.

With the young offenders having been moved and the girls to go soon, that left only the men. There would be absolutely no chance for education for them. I believed that among the six hundred or so, there had to be at least a couple who would be there forever until they would be able to have a trial. I could help by offering those who were between the ages of eighteen and twenty-one the courses from the Volunteer for Independent Learning. I talked to the program coordinator at the West. She agreed to clear me to be the volunteer coordinator as she knew I would be safe to have inside the institution.

Thus, I became the official teacher who talked to the men who wanted to take a high school course. I continued to be known only as Barb. I could go to their range if they requested and could talk only through the large bars at the entry way to their range. This permission was granted by the CO on duty for the area and then only if there were no trouble on that range. It was fortunate that most of the COs knew me and that I had a reputation for being a no-nonsense person. The men were to be seen one at a time. We would first discuss their educational backgrounds and wishes. I tried to direct them to a subject in which there was a chance for their success. We aimed for those courses, such as English, needed for a high school graduation certificate. They paid forty dollars for each course. I was allowed to get the needed money from their personal accounts in the office. As before all work and results could be transferred to any provincial institution where the sentence was to be done. The staff there knew me and they were most accommodating. I went into the jail one day each week, usually on a Tuesday. I looked first to see if there were new requests and then checked my mailbox for new material and marked work. Most men were serious; we were both happy to see the marks in the eighties and nineties. Also there were other days with the exams to supervise. That required my being there, and setting up the time and finding free space. Exams could be done outside or at another jail.

I said before, I found the people facing these charges such as murder to be most interesting. Here are some cases I was aware of this time. Circumstances and names are changed. One young boy was with me as a student long enough to complete several of his grade 12 academic courses. His marks were very high, and the comments of the markers had been most complimentary. So what was the problem? He had been just one person in a group when they were all partying. In the morning one of those participants was dead. There was one identifiable possession left behind; it was his. They arrested him. He refused to rat! He resisted the pressure for months and finally agreed to accept a lesser charge. I wonder what ever happened to him.

Another man who was also accused of murder was also putting in time. He tried to take a course, but was not really interested. He knew he would have a heavy sentence and just wanted something to read. Finally, he explained to me that he had had very little education as he had spent his elementary years down in the furnace room smoking with the janitor. He was a native from Ontario, and one could guess that the courts did not know what to do with him. I was able to remove the hardcover from a book about his native heritage, and I think he did try to read it. There was another man with whom the courts did not know how to deal. His case we could read about in the newspapers. His charge would have involved sending him to an American state that has the death penalty. If our government knew that they were not our citizens, they could not have a course.

Most of the men who were serious and who completed work knew that theirs would be a sentence of a reasonable length. They believed they would be able to have the marks count toward their graduation certificates. It was rewarding to see their enthusiasm and progress. They were friendly and respectful. Once, a student even apologized as he was embarrassed that I had to hear such foul language. Did I learn some interesting new swearwords? Not really, they were the words I had heard from the girls, particularly the most common one can be used for any part of speech and frequently was! One soon becomes immune to it. Now, it only really bothers me to hear God's name used in vain, and I honestly did not hear that much in jail. The inmates who had had any religious background would not allow it. The men were different from the girls in behavior though. I was treated like a lady. I had the feeling they were seeing the gray hair and thinking of me as a mother.

I heard about their children and about how they really did want to change so their offspring would have better lives. That wish was expressed more by the men than by the girls. Analyze that one! I saw a lot of large muscles. For their spare time there were not enough books to read, so exercise either outside in yard or in the range did pass the time. It was preferable to gambling. I saw beautiful very professional tattoos and a few "homemade" jail tattoos. Some men had tattoos in brilliant colors such a pink and green; the girls usually only had the small black ones. Who really makes the most spending money from crime!

All forms of independence are personally very important to me, especially financial! I knew a lot of the girls believed they had no choice but to do what they were told. The big surprise was that a lot of the men were in that the same position. When incarcerated, they sometimes had people of power controlling them. This certainly applied to the terrorists I knew and to the members of large gangs. In some cases, it was just like the movies. One the young offenders had been a member of the Tigers of Sri Lanka fame. He had been forced to drive the getaway car as he would not be charged as an adult. He did not even have a driver's license!

I had learned and changed a lot! I now fully appreciated that the guilty people truly should be punished! Most of them knew that and expected it. Regarding my experience with the women as well, I changed in that I no longer thought all "criminals" should be totally regarded as lowlife. I did, however, meet men who were scary. I had seen such faces on the outside too. They have a cold look in their eyes. I avoid them. Here, I did meet a man who had a charge that I honestly find revolting. He asked for a course, and I saw no real reason to deny him. He stayed a long time and we got to know each other, and even he was at least likeable. I could understand and like the good part of his personality.

Overall, I guess I did change for the better . . . I think. I left that job when the provincial government stopped all ILC courses at any detention center. Again, what a false economy!

Chapter 16

Part 1: TLC Afterward

What did I teach? I taught whatever was required to keep my job! Often it was necessary to take extra courses in a different subject area to do that.

What did I learn? One always learns far more than anticipated when working in a job that involves communication with people. I came to realize that teaching was about far more than controlling a class by fear. I learned students were just immature adults, some more mature than others! No matter their age, they wanted to know that they were worthwhile beings and wanted to prove that to me and to themselves.

What changes have I seen? I personally changed a lot from that ignorant, arrogant, but eager novitiate who thought she knew everything and exactly how to teach it. I gradually realized how much I had to learn not only about teaching but also about myself. Gradually I realized that absolutely nothing is as important to me or to any student and any other person as *love*. It can change things and perceptions and knowledge. *But* that happens only by using a lot of the desirable characteristic most teacher do possess and practice: patience, faith in others, and courage to try unique and nonthreatening approaches. These traits develop with experience and the proper training of teachers.

What I am discussing in this book is really more than my biography. It is a history of the gradual changes in education in the provinces in which I was employed. Did you notice that I began by working in a school ruled by fear? Now, I would look for my personal satisfaction and looked for the development in my students of their own desire to learn what they need to have personally satisfactory lives. At the end, I saw myself an equal and a partner to both students and administrators. This scenario changed very slowly. Witness the happy, friendly young staff at Emery compared with a recent horror story about one present-day high school. There the principal is afraid of the gangs in his school. The teachers are suffering in this poisoned atmosphere because he has accepted that fear, not love, should be in the feeling in the school.

Of course, one of the biggest of changes has been in the effectiveness and growth of the Teachers Federations; they are now like trade unions. Their hard-won economic benefits negated my need to go work after I retired as my father had done. I will be eternally grateful. There are now too many qualified teachers and in new negotiations are ahead. Will teachers be called upon to give up some of these hard-won advances? I hate to think that it might all go back to the bad financial situation of my father's time.

The life of educational administrators has changed a lot. Now, having the use of computers, the administrators have hit of the idea of having a semester system, which means many more individual student timetables. In high school, to get the required number of hours for each course, all courses are evaluated as being equal, and thus given the same ninety minutes time slot. It is far better in the long run for the progress of individual students. Essentially, many high schools are now ungraded.

There are now certain requirements which must be completed in four years to gain the precious grade 12 graduation certificate.

Those certificates are required for even the most elementary level job training, or further study. There are different expected achievement levels in each subject. Thus, when entering high school, each student basically has his/her own timetable. They each progress by their own efforts, and levels of ability, not by age. Also, students can now advance more rapidly by taking computer courses anytime and/or by going to summer and night schools. Such individualization can require many more hours for some more challenged student. Consequently, we have students whose levels of school successes vary greatly. There are the students who cannot pass some of the government-required English and math tests. Unfortunately, of course, they do pass because of the "kindness" of the administrators! How do we solve these problems: illegal dropouts and students who now hold these worthless certificates? In previous times, they could hope to get a manual job. Add this new "no job" frustration to the many other sources of student frustration! Is all this not what is causing the current state of serious discipline problems in some areas? Is that not why we must have policemen stationed in the worst schools? The answer has to be earlier individualized instruction. It is too late to start individual instruction at grade 9 level.

Part 2: Necessary Changes Needed in Education

I am writing this at the end of the end of August when newspapers are full of ideas for improving the present Ontario system of education. These ideas are in response to the obvious failures of the present schools to deliver desired results. It would appear that revision is needed. Most educators have ideas for improving this situation. The following are my ideas. Other educators, I am sure, could add to this list. It is time for serious adjustments. It is not time for just more talk!

1. The old system of arranging all students by age groups in elementary schools should be eliminated.

Currently these administrators are urged to do social promotion by age. Thus the grade group becomes a social unit, and all are passed on to the next grade regardless of abilities or successes. It certainly meant my having those unfortunate illiterate children in a special grade 9 English class. They hated reading and writing. Yet how could they now get a job as reading is required with the ever increasing computer use in even for the lowest paid positions? If classes were homogeneous for ability and subject background, instead of by birthdays, then there could be more meaningful group instruction and hope for success for all. It is that which could lead to improved self-esteem. Every student needs to believe that he/she can cope with the study the material that is presented. Does anyone really believe that the other students did not know? Did not all those failing classmates hear dumb or worse? That was what was damaging to that child's ego and self-confidence!

A new system can be possible whereby the individual could progress at his/her own pace through his/her education from kindergarten to employment or onto further education. Maybe he/she would learn skills for a chosen career! Would that be an improvement not only for the individual but also for our society as well? Classes would be very mixed by ages, and it would be more like family groups, resembling the old-fashioned country school. There, students accepted and helped other! Each child would have his/her own computer-created timetable and proceed at his/her own rate in each subject. I was very dyslexic and dyspraxic. At a very early age, my mother, a teacher, recognized my problem and worked with me many summers for reading and spelling. Therefore, at a young age I could probably have passed reading tests at what is now the grade 2 level. I was hopeless in numeracy, so I would have been in the first class for arithmetic much longer. These two subjects are essential unfortunately! I would have made great progress in art and music! Physical education was always a great trial, but in each of these different classes I would have felt accepted and have been encouraged.

2. There should be many levels and types of programs for teacher education.

The Province of Ontario has just announced an increase of time for training for educators—horrors! Especially if this means more of the same boring lectures. One year was enough! Consider some of these radical ideas:

In many fields of work, there are different levels of training, of ability, and of pay among the workers. We see this in health care and in businesses. Why not in education? Why must every teacher have two degrees? The system used to operate very efficiently with those who had only one year of what was called teachers' college professional training. Do many years of schooling make a person a better teacher? In fact, it often seems that the more education a person has, the more the person tends to believe, as I did at first, that I was a superior being because of my degrees. Generally, these people do not work successfully with the youngest or the handicapped children. In those cases the teacher should be

T. L. C.

compassionate, loving, and encouraging. Really, children, like
dogs, are quick to sense dislike. Nothing is more threatening
than knowing that you are both disliked and misunderstood.
Compassionate and understanding people with the training in the
social sciences should be successful teachers or teachers' aides. I
have a friend with two degrees who spent her career working as
a teacher's aide where she felt useful and fulfilled. Many social
science graduates would probable feel the same. They could just
enjoy the children and not worry about the total responsibility of
large groups. To become a teacher's aide, a one-year course or even
courses taken as part of the first degree, should be sufficient. Think
of the middle-aged women who have raised families and who
would love this opportunity. They might not wish for a full course
load but could do one year. How about adding to the mix a few
retired people as volunteers? The most important help for teaching
reading is someone who will listen and encourage a child as he/she
sounds out the letters. Older people doing this volunteering have
found a bond that both participants appreciated.

I am, of course, suggesting a large number of adults in each
classroom. It will not be in the old "seats in rows and be silent"
place. Each student will be learning with the appropriate help. All
pupils will feel comfortable as they will all be at approximately the
same achievement level in that particular subject. There will be
many different ages of students and helpers. Creating this positive
atmosphere is the master teacher's job, and he/she will be the
only leader in each room. I have heard of one experimental school
in Hamilton City where they do not refer at all to the students
as being in a certain grade. In the upper grades there is now, in
downtown Toronto, an effective monitoring system. Volunteer
help is offered by professional office workers in their free time.
Elementary schools often welcome volunteer help now. Our
suburbs need these programs as we have so many students for
whom English is the second language.

| 95 |

3. Educators should be making as much use as possible of all available technology.

Some educational leaders are waking up to the importance and need for utilizing new technology. It is what the students themselves would call a no-brainer. We keep hearing and seeing on television of the wonderful learning in these experimental classes where devices such as iPads are in use. All who are involved are so enthusiastic! Why cannot it be done more in high schools? Think of what could be accomplished in all classes. In mathematics, the Khan programs could be used; they are available to all and are free! Also free at the present time are the MOOC courses. They are massively open online courses that cover every conceivable field of knowledge and are often taught by university professors. Anyone can sign up. Think of all the fields of study that would thus be available to all students. One could then write real research papers that involve real research. The teacher could oversee the collation of facts. Then he would watch how the student arranged the information for the finished report, a report done on the student's own computer! That report could honestly be the student's own original presentation. It could eliminate the cheating now common.

Making use of current technology does not just apply to high schools but also to universities. The Khan courses are designed so that the student can review the material if it had not been clear the first time. Should the confusion persist, then an adult in the room would help. The master teacher would be available for extra help with difficulties. For the younger ages, teachers could feel that they were making an important contribution. It appeared that, in the experimental technology classes, the atmosphere was more friendly, encouraging, and loving than in the traditional classroom. Students really do want to work and to be successful. As in the old saying: success breeds not only success but also self-confidence. Successful students are more apt to lead happy and contributing lives. Those extra adults could prevent a current problem: the playing games instead of actual learning from their own computers.

These are the arguments that they can foretell against these changes:

First, I am advocating major and startling changes. Yes, and I am serious. The major complaint will be the cost, but what is it now costing our total economy to have educational systems that are not functioning? If iPads are considered as too expensive, think of the cost of using all the old outdated printed textbooks. Students deserve updated information. The electronic devices would actually be cheaper than text replacements. Education administrators must begin to do what is called thinking outside the box. Today it is the private schools that are doing these changes. It is the parents who pay. The children who chose to go to public schools are underprivileged.

Secondly, students also will have to be helped to understand these new ideas. This, however, will involve just one of the many changes they will be forced to make in their lives. The technological revolution is fast moving. All people, not just students, will need to be helped to keep up. If not, we will create another poor class of citizens that the tech-savvy will be required to support. If that happens, there will be much personal suffering! Individually, all people must be prepared to do the new learning and relearning. This will enable us to meet the inevitable changes and challenges. Life is more than the tests faced in a school.

A third complaint will be that most people will not change. They will if forced to, especially if there is a salary or a financial deficit attached to nonconformance! We saw such great progress and such great changes following the industrial revolution. It is time we all realized that we really are experiencing another evolution. We had better change and adapt as quickly as possible. A good example occurred when I made these suggestions to a number of fellow teachers. "I would not have any other adults in my classroom." In other words I liked being in control! They could still be a boss. The circumstances would be just very different!

The first countries to improve the situation by focusing on the education of each person, instead of group education, will be the new world leader. Guess who was *not* the world leader in math scores? It is China! That was a shock. Their pupils progress by age groups. Now, they are experimenting in education to see how best to evaluate teachers and how best to do student testing. We should be doing the same but much more. The country that changes and improves education first will quickly change its economy. It will provide its citizens with health, wealth, and more fulfilled lives— lives with more free time for individual learning and pursuit of personal creative interests.

With a changed educational system, there can be unforeseeable progress in many fields of endeavor. Maybe, there will even be progress in learning to live together on a potentially crowded planet. Maybe we will all become more loving, will think, and will spend fewer of our resources on killing each other. Maybe, we will think more about how to help each other. One of my friends who had been involved in education called me Plato when she heard my ideas. I consider that a compliment!